THINKING KID
MATH
Learning Fun for Growing Minds!

K

Thinkings Kids™
Carson-Dellosa Publishing LLC
Greensboro, North Carolina

Thinking Kids™
Carson-Dellosa Publishing LLC
P.O. Box 35665
Greensboro, NC 27425 USA

ISBN 978-1-4838-0204-6

Table of Contents

Welcome to *Thinking Kids™ Math!* This book contains everything you and your child need for hands-on learning and math practice. It gives you the tools to help fill knowledge gaps and build foundations that will prepare your child for higher-level math. Your child will learn to think about, know, apply, and reason with math concepts.

Thinking Kids™ Math is organized into five sections based on the skills covered. Each activity supports the Common Core State Standards and offers a fun and active approach to essential kindergarten math skills. Interactive lessons and the use of manipulatives build a concrete example of math concepts to help your child develop mathematical understanding.

Work through the interactive activities with your child using manipulatives around your house. Guide your child through each activity, and then allow them to perform the activity with little or no support.

Examples of common household items you could substitute for counters or blocks are different colored buttons, paper clips, pennies, and dice. A variety of manipulatives in different colors, sizes, textures, and shapes is essential to your child's learning. It is important for them to interact with different types of manipulatives so they do not associate certain concepts with certain manipulatives.

Thinking Kids™ Math promotes the use of manipulatives to engage and challenge your child. The interaction with manipulatives promotes motor skills and exploration while engaging your child in hands-on experience. Activities also call for children to draw, use tally marks, pictures, and graphic organizers. After children have worked with manipulatives, they transfer their understanding of the concept by drawing pictures in place of the manipulatives.

Each activity supports early learning standards and challenges your child's critical thinking and problem solving skills. In *Thinking Kids™ Math*, your child will learn about:

- Numbers and Counting
- Addition and Subtraction
- Patterns
- Shapes and Attributes
- Measurement
- Sorting and Graphing

Jelly Bean Count

Count the jelly beans in each jar. Write the number.

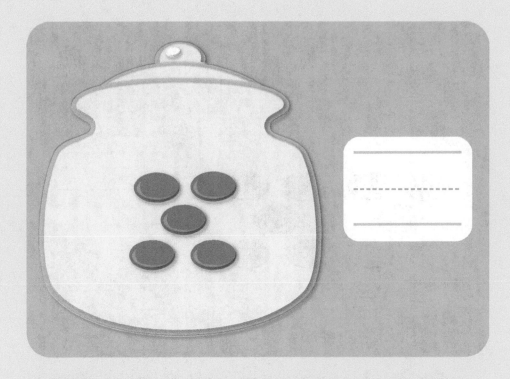

Count the jelly beans in each jar. Write the number.

Put a counter on each balloon in the first set as you count it. Then, move the counters to the next set to count the balloons.

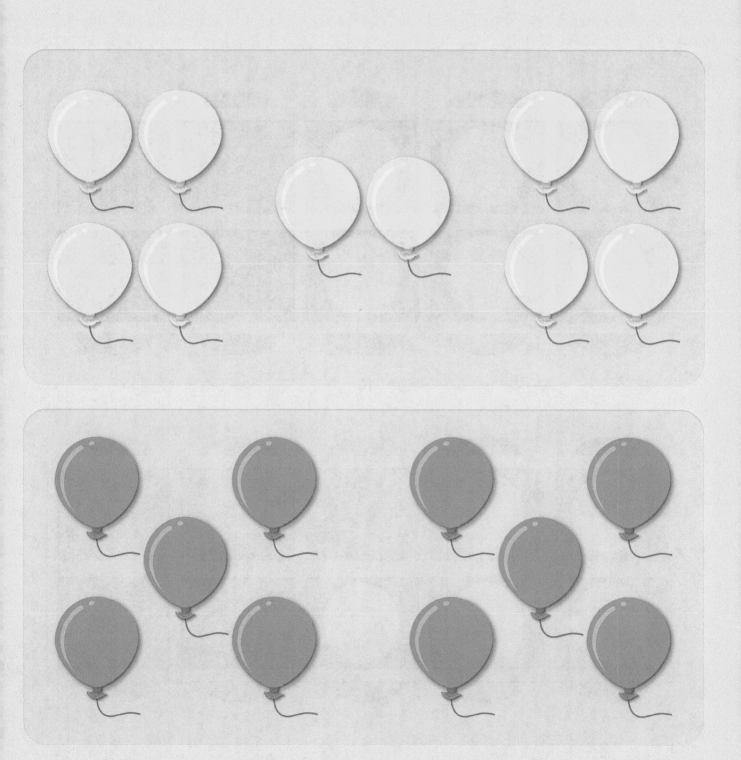

Put one counter on each place mat that has a circle. Count how many people will sit at each table.

Put one counter on each place mat that has a circle. Count how many people will sit at each table.

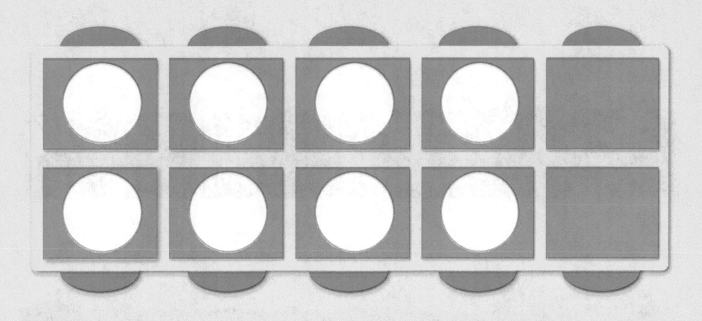

Carrot Patch

Plant carrots in each row to show the number on the sign. Use cubes or counters.

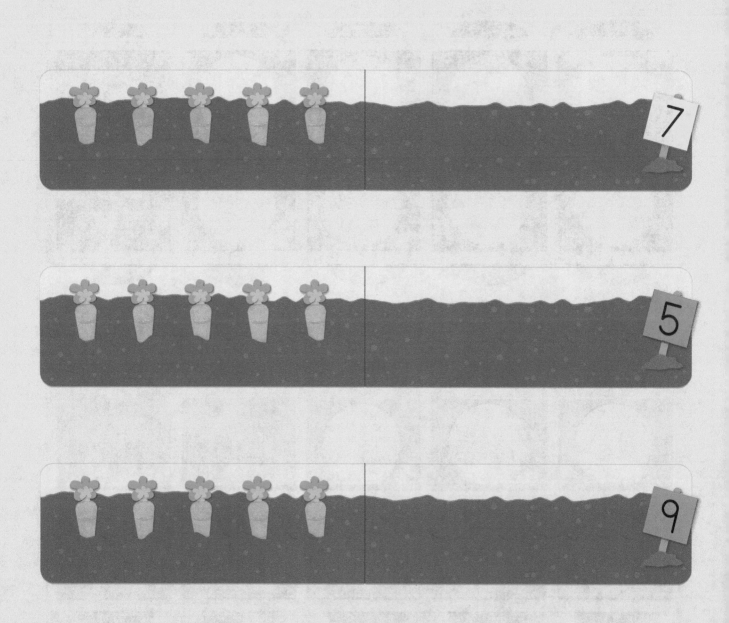

Plant carrots in each row to show the number on the sign. Use cubes or counters.

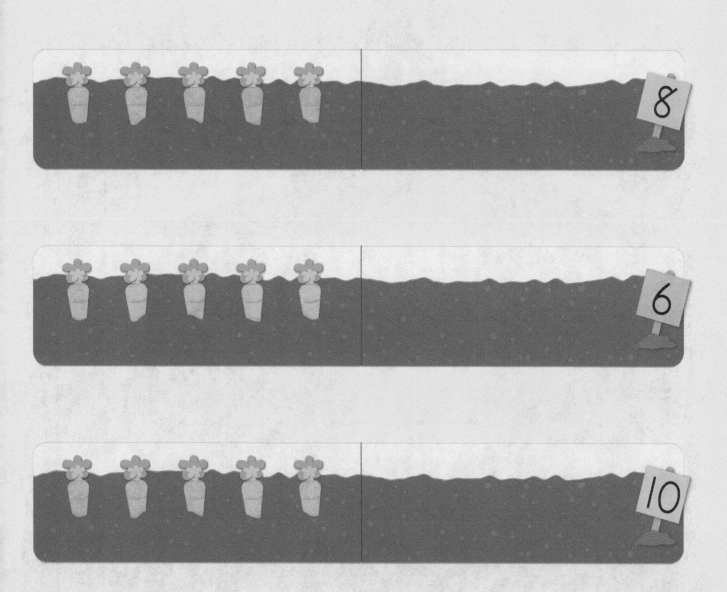

Put 10 sheep in the barn. Use counters. Put the rest outside of the barn. Count how many are outside.

Put 10 horses in the barn. Use counters. Put the rest outside of the barn. Count how many are outside.

On the Farm

Put 10 cows in the barn. Use counters. Put the rest outside of the barn. Count how many are outside.

Put 10 sheep in the barn. Use counters. Put the rest outside of the barn. Count how many are outside.

Take a handful of apples and put them on the tree. Use counters.
Move the apples to the ten frames. Count how many total apples.

Put a block on each flower. Move the blocks to the ten frames.
Count how many total flowers.

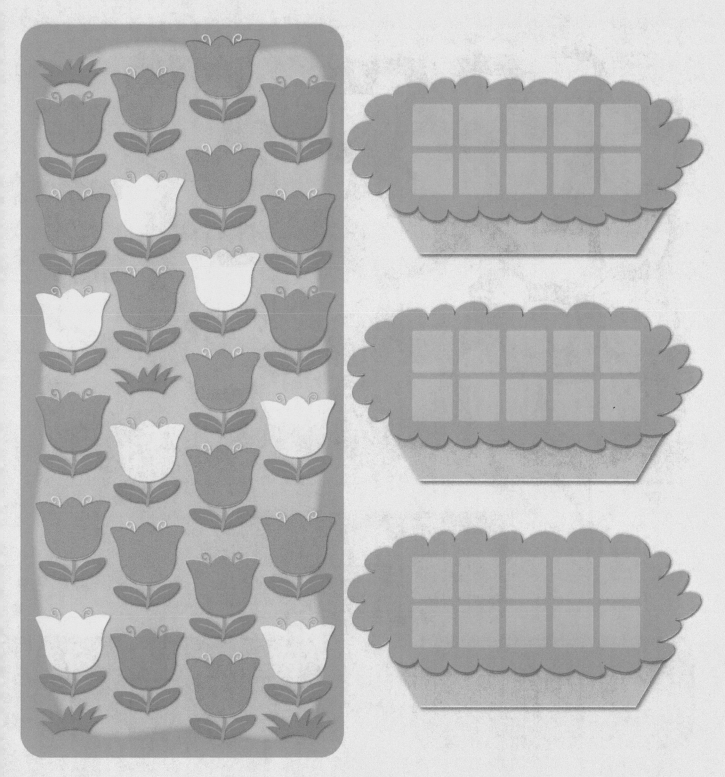

Ducks in a Pond

Put a block on each duck. Move the blocks to the ten frames.
Count how many total ducks.

Frogs on Logs

Write the missing number or numbers on each log.

Frogs on Logs

Write the missing number or numbers on each log.

_____ 2 3

1 _____ 3 4 _____

Write the missing number or numbers on each log.

1 ___ 3 ___

1 2 3 ___

Frogs on Logs

Write the missing number or numbers on each log.

Write the number of each ant's place in line. Some have been done for you.

Ants Go Marching

Write the number of each ant's place in line. Some have been done for you.

Write the number of each ant's place in line. Some have been done for you.

Ants Go Marching

Write the number of each ant's place in line. Some have been done for you.

Put one matching colored cube on each train car. Then, answer the questions.

What color is each car?

1st _____

3rd _____

6th _____

8th _____

Put one matching colored cube on each train car. Then, answer the questions.

What color is each car?

2nd

_____

4th

_____

5th

_____

9th

_____

© Carson-Dellosa
CD-704461

Write the number of each bear's place if he is going down to the red door.

Bears on the Stairs

Write the number for each bear's place if he is going up to the blue door.

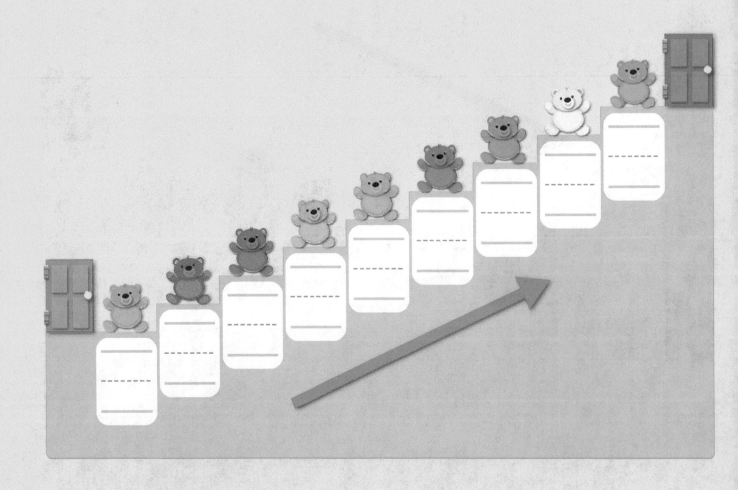

Count the objects in each pair of boxes. Under each box, write the number to tell how many. Circle the box that shows more objects.

Count the objects in each pair of boxes. Under each box, write the number to tell how many. Circle the box that shows less objects.

Count the objects in each pair of boxes. Under each box, write the number to tell how many. Circle the box that shows more objects.

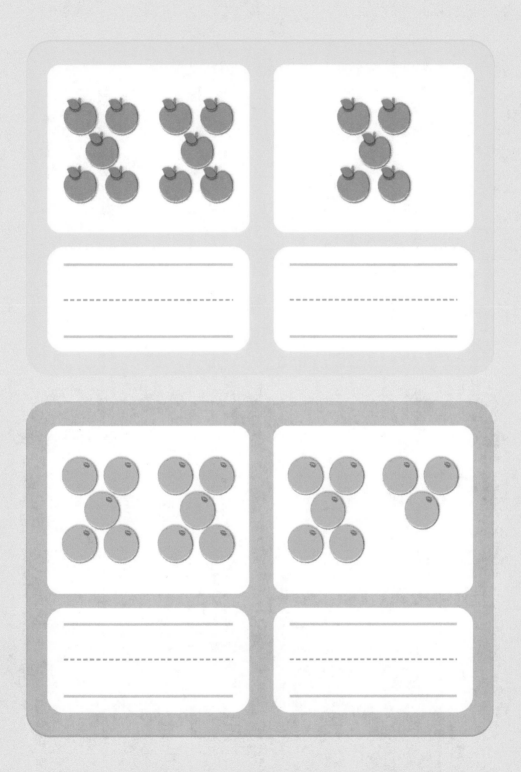

Show Less

Count the objects in each pair of boxes. Under each box, write the number to tell how many. Circle the box that shows less objects.

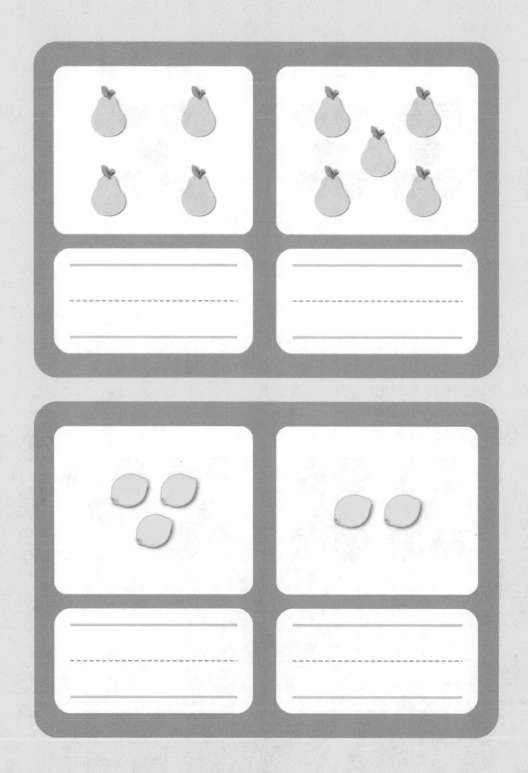

Put 10 fish in the first fish tank. Use counters. Put 7 fish in the second fish tank. Write each number. Then, circle more or less.

more   less

Put a handful of fish in the first fish tank. Use counters. Put more or less fish in the second fish tank. Write each number. Then, circle more or less.

less   more   more   less

Circle the dog in each pair that has more spots.

Circle the dog in each pair that has less spots.

Roll a die. Put that number of eggs in the middle nest. Use counters. Put less eggs in the first nest and more eggs in the last nest. Write each number.

less   more

Ladybug Spots

Count the spots on each ladybug. Write the number.

Roll two dice. Draw that number of spots on the first ladybug. Write the number. Repeat for the second ladybug.

Ladybug Spots

Roll two dice. Draw that number of spots on the first ladybug. Write the number. Use counters to show different ways to make that same number on the other ladybugs. Draw the spots.

Count the rocks in each collector's box. Write the number.

Rock Collector

Count the rocks in each collector's box. Write the number.

Roll the die. Put that number of rocks in the first collector's box. Write the number. Repeat for the other collector's box.

Count the cookies. Write the number. Put that number of counters in the ten frame.

Drop 10 cookies onto the jar. Use counters. Move the cookies that land on the jar to the ten frame. Count the cookies and write the number.

How Many Crackers?

Count the crackers on the plate. Write the number and the number word.

Roll 3 dice. Count that many crackers and put them on the plate. Use counters. Move the crackers to the ten frames. Write the number and the number word.

Count the objects in each pair of boxes. Under each box, write the number to tell how many. Circle same or different.

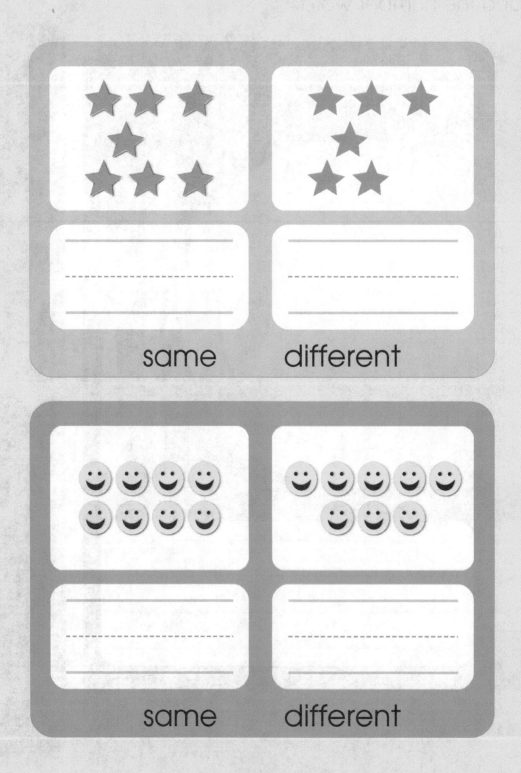

same   different

same   different

Count the objects in each pair of boxes. Under each box, write the number to tell how many. Circle same or different.

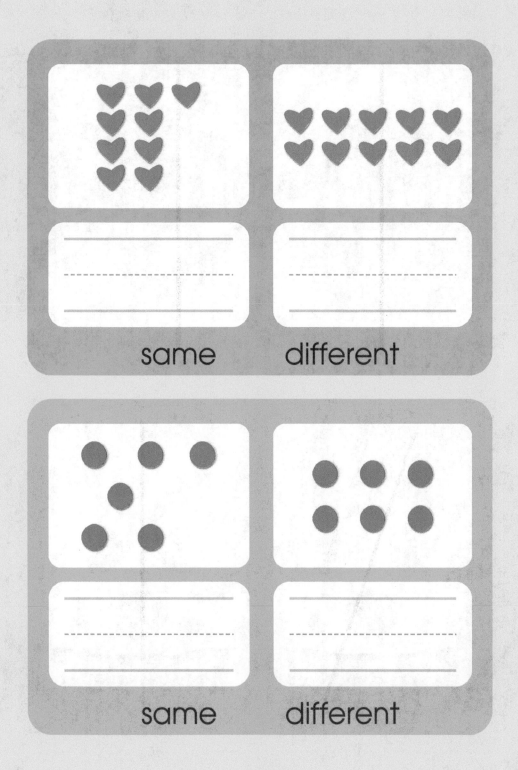

same   different

same   different

Look at each pair of foods. Circle the food in each pair that shows equal parts.

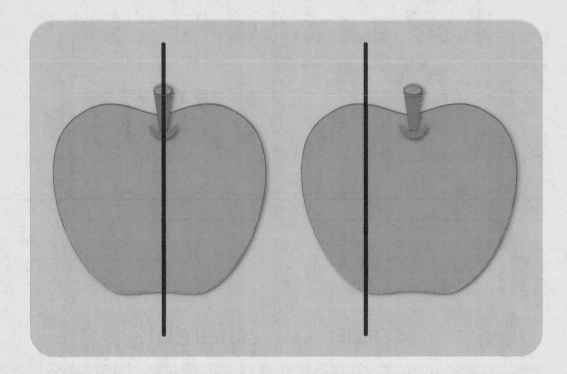

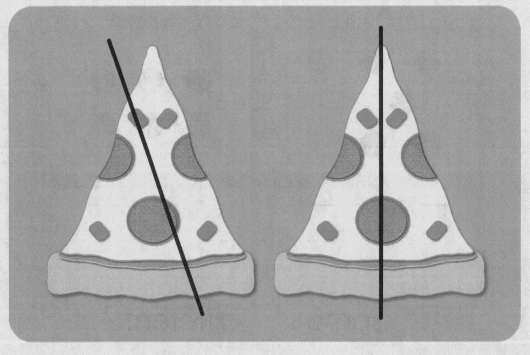

Circle the sandwich that shows equal parts. In the second box, draw a line on the cracker to show equal parts.

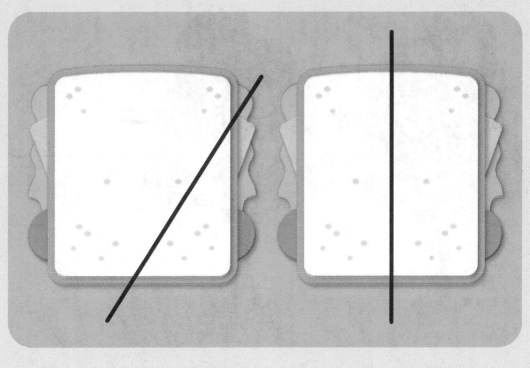

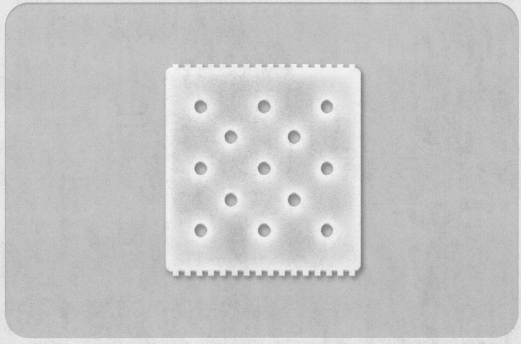

Apple Tree Addition

Put counters on the apples in each tree. Count the apples. Write how many apples in all.

Put counters on the apples in each tree. Count the apples. Write how many apples in all.

Domino Addition

Put a domino in each box. Count the dots on each half of the domino. Write the numbers on the lines. Add the numbers and write the sum.

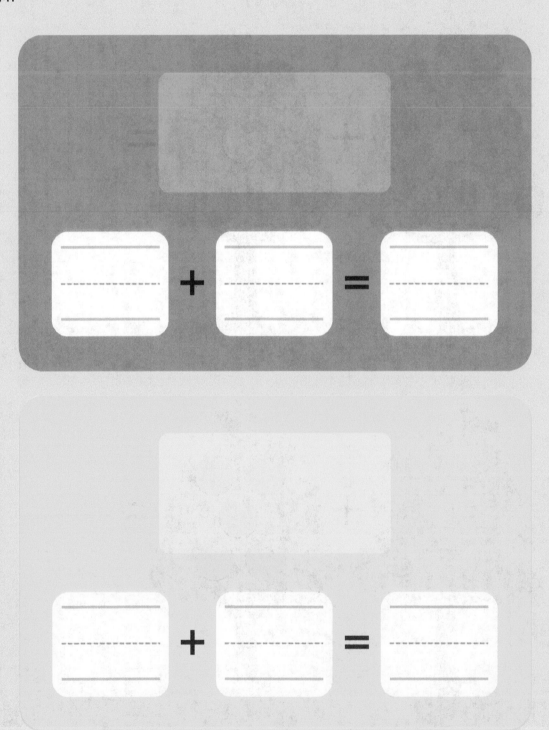

Domino Addition

Put a domino in each box. Count the dots on each half of the domino. Write the numbers on the lines. Add the numbers and write the sum.

Put 10 pieces of popcorn on the first bag. Roll a die and move that number of pieces from the first bag to the second bag. Write the number sentence to show how many pieces are left. Repeat 3 times.

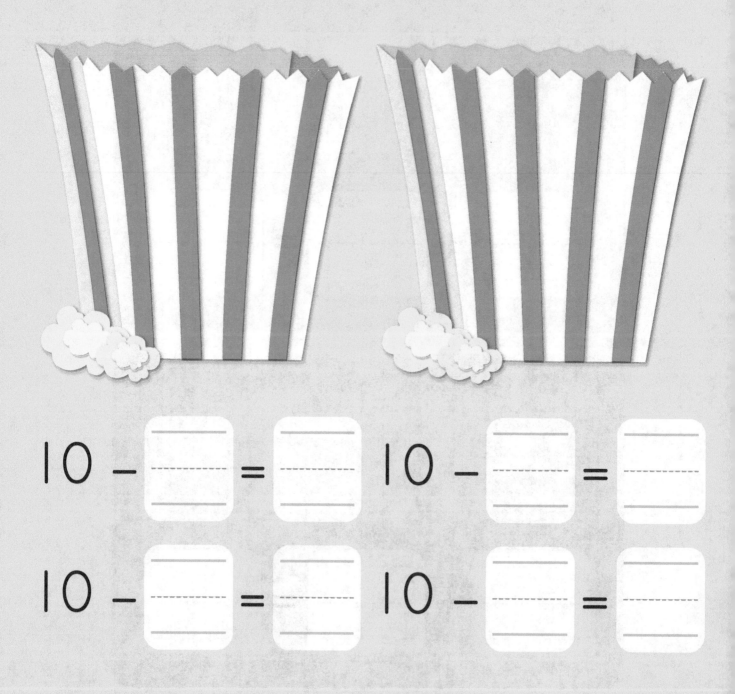

$10 - \underline{\hspace{2cm}} = \underline{\hspace{2cm}}$ $10 - \underline{\hspace{2cm}} = \underline{\hspace{2cm}}$

$10 - \underline{\hspace{2cm}} = \underline{\hspace{2cm}}$ $10 - \underline{\hspace{2cm}} = \underline{\hspace{2cm}}$

Put 15 pieces of popcorn on the first bag. Roll a die and move that number of pieces from the first bag to the second bag. Write the number sentence to show how many pieces are left. Repeat 3 times.

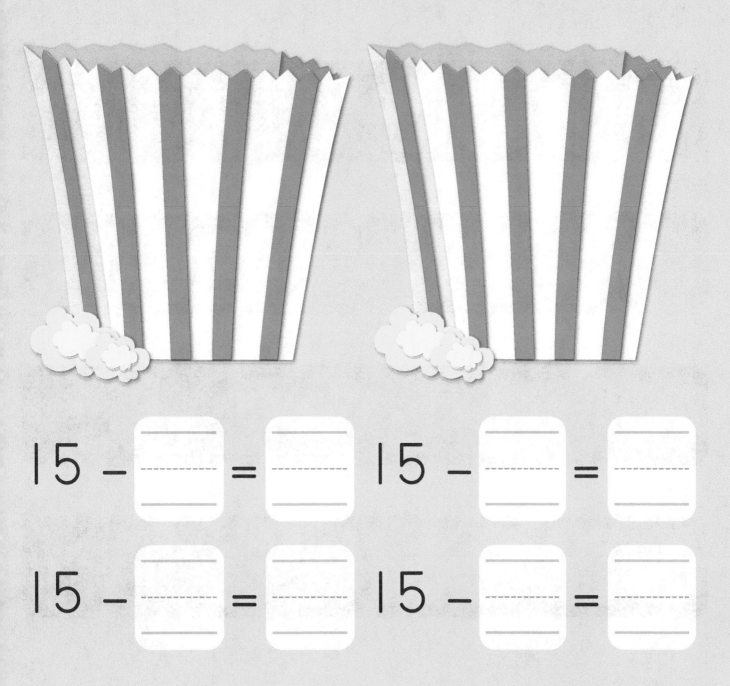

15 − _____ = _____   15 − _____ = _____

15 − _____ = _____   15 − _____ = _____

Pumpkin Patch

Cross out pumpkins so that only 2 pumpkins are left in each row.

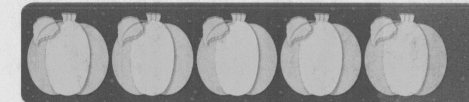

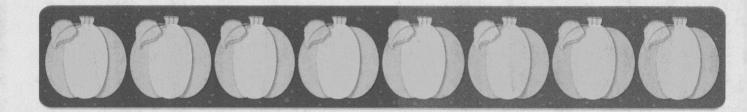

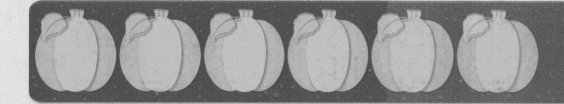

Cross out pumpkins so that only 3 pumpkins are left in each row.

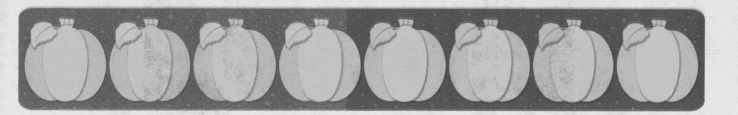

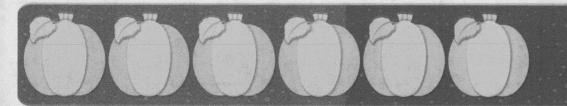

Acro-bots

Use two colors of cubes to show a sum of 4. Write the number sentence. Flip the stack and write the new number sentence.

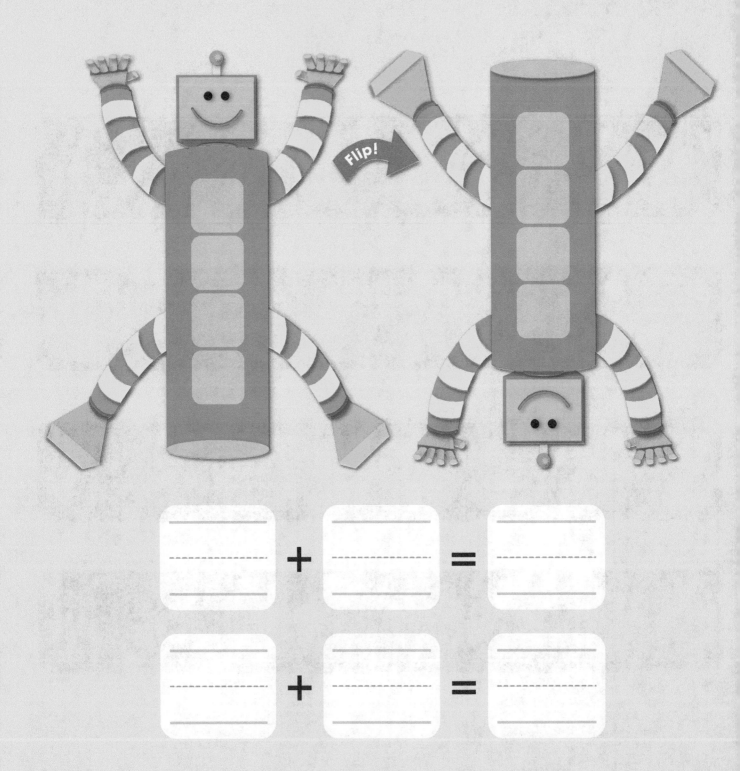

_____ + _____ = _____

_____ + _____ = _____

Use two colors of cubes to show a sum of 5. Write the number sentence. Flip the stack and write the new number sentence.

_____ + _____ = _____

_____ + _____ = _____

Hopping Along

Use the number line to solve each problem. Write each answer.

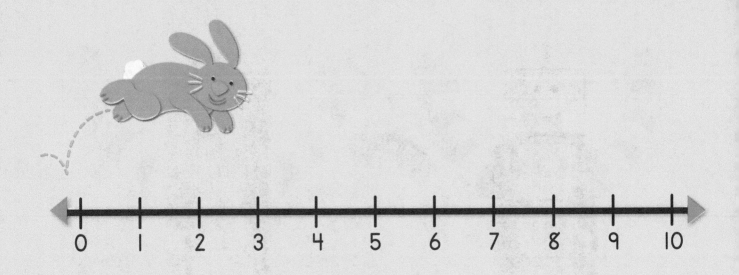

$$2 + 2 = $$

$$7 - 4 = $$

$$9 - 4 = $$

Use the number line to solve each problem. Write each answer.

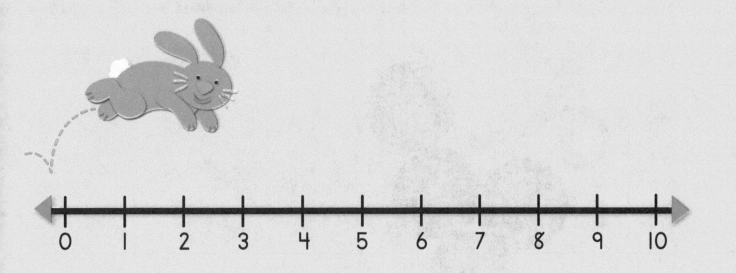

1 + 7 =

8 – 2 =

10 – 3 =

Bunches of Grapes

Count the grapes in each bunch. Add grapes to each bunch to make a total of 10.

CD-704461

Count the grapes in each bunch. Add grapes to each bunch to make a total of 10.

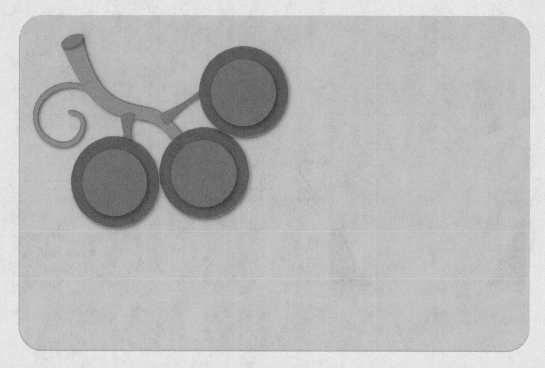

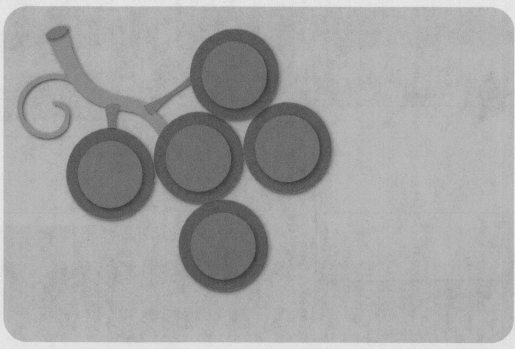

Draw the missing crayons in each box. Count all of the crayons in each box. Write the sum.

$$2 + 5 = \underline{\hspace{2cm}}$$

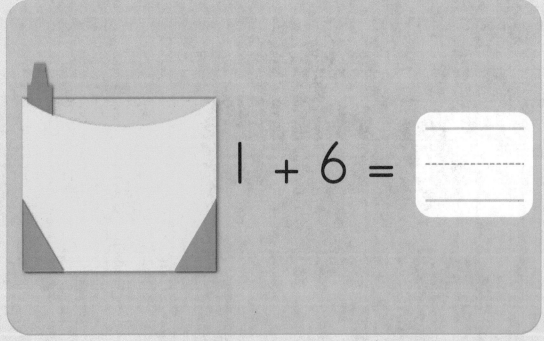

$$1 + 6 = \underline{\hspace{2cm}}$$

Draw the missing crayons in each box. Count all of the crayons in each box. Write the sum.

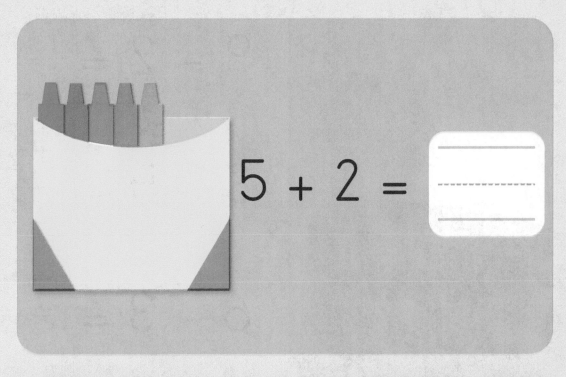

$5 + 2 =$

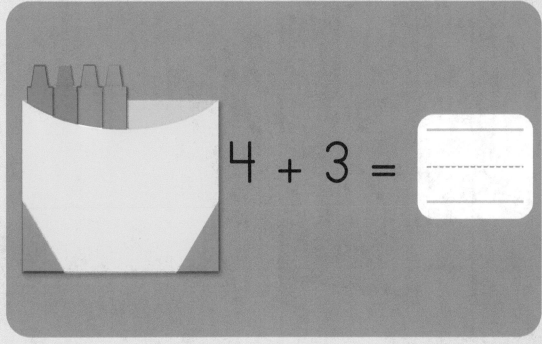

$4 + 3 =$

Treasure Chest

Put gems in the chest to show each problem. Write the number of gems left in the chest.

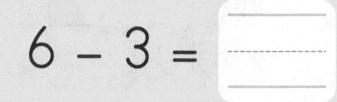

$$9 - 2 = \underline{\hspace{3cm}}$$

$$8 - 4 = \underline{\hspace{3cm}}$$

$$6 - 3 = \underline{\hspace{3cm}}$$

Put gems in the chest to show each problem. Write the number of gems left in the chest.

$$7 - 2 = \underline{}$$

$$8 - 2 = \underline{}$$

$$9 - 8 = \underline{}$$

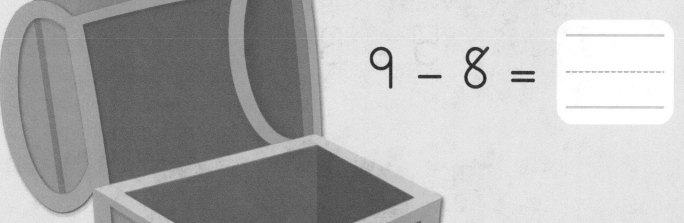

Squirrel Subtraction

Each squirrel ate some acorns. Cross out the number of acorns that each squirrel ate. Write how many acorns are left.

5 - 3 =

8 - 2 =

Each squirrel ate some acorns. Cross out the number of acorns that each squirrel ate. Write how many acorns are left.

$7 - 4 =$ ____

$6 - 1 =$ ____

© Carson-Dellosa
CD-704461

Count by 2s. Write the numbers. Then, circle the numbers on the chart that you counted.

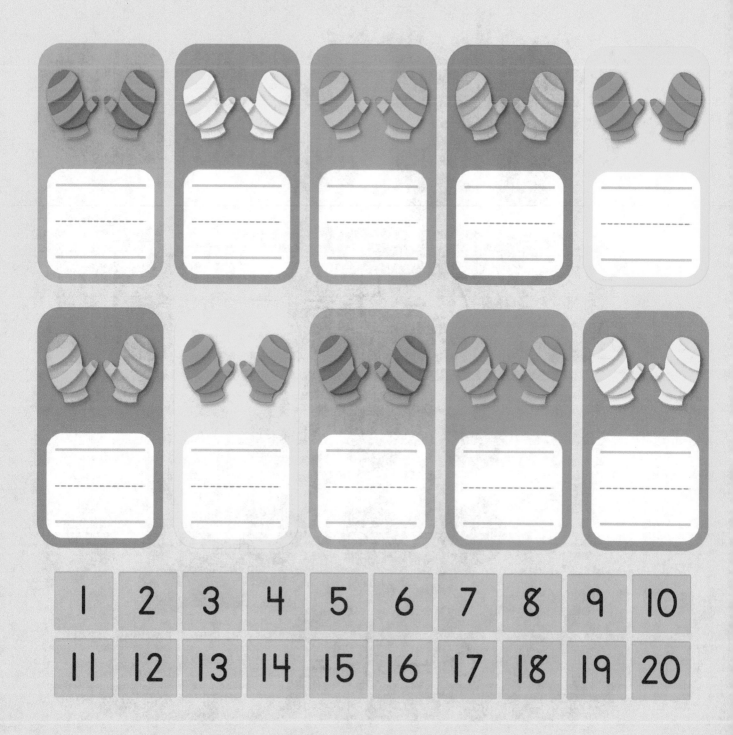

Circle each pair of shoes. Then, answer the questions.

How many children? _____

How many shoes? _____

Pairs of Shoes

Circle each pair of shoes. Then, answer the questions.

How many children? _____

How many shoes? _____

Count by 5s. Write the numbers. Then, circle the numbers on the chart that you counted.

1	2	3	4	5	6	7	8	9	10
11	12	13	14	15	16	17	18	19	20
21	22	23	24	25	26	27	28	29	30

Circle the groups of 5 in each set of fruit. Write how many groups of 5 you circled. Write how many objects in all.

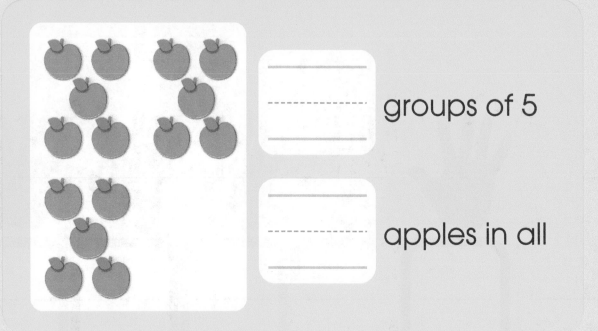

------------- groups of 5

------------- apples in all

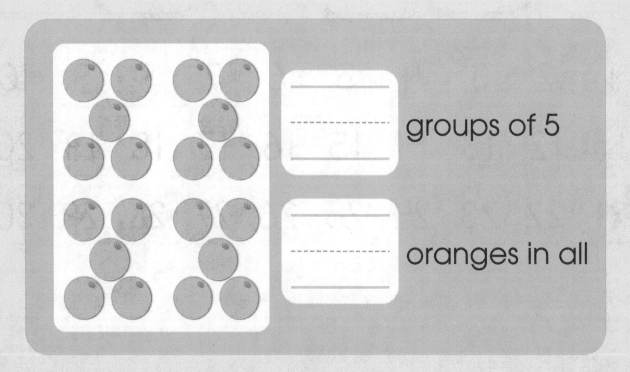

------------- groups of 5

------------- oranges in all

Circle the groups of 5 in each set of fruit. Write how many groups of 5 you circled. Write how many objects in all.

_____ groups of 5

_____ pears in all

_____ groups of 5

_____ lemons in all

Count by 10s. Write the numbers. Then, circle the numbers on the chart that you counted.

1	2	3	4	5	6	7	8	9	10
11	12	13	14	15	16	17	18	19	20
21	22	23	24	25	26	27	28	29	30
31	32	33	34	35	36	37	38	39	40
41	42	43	44	45	46	47	48	49	50

Complete the chart by counting to 100.

1		3		5		7		9	
11		13		15		17		19	
21		23		25		27		29	
31		33		35		37		39	
41		43		45		47		49	
51		53		55		57		59	
61		63		65		67		69	
71		73		75		77		79	
81		83		85		87		89	
91		93		95		97		99	

Complete the chart by counting to 100.

	2		4		6		8		10
	12		14		16		18		20
	22		24		26		28		30
	32		34		36		38		40
	42		44		46		48		50
	52		54		56		58		60
	62		64		66		68		70
	72		74		76		78		80
	82		84		86		88		90
	92		94		96		98		100

Circle the groups of 10 pins in each set. Write how many groups of 10 you circled. Write how many pins in all.

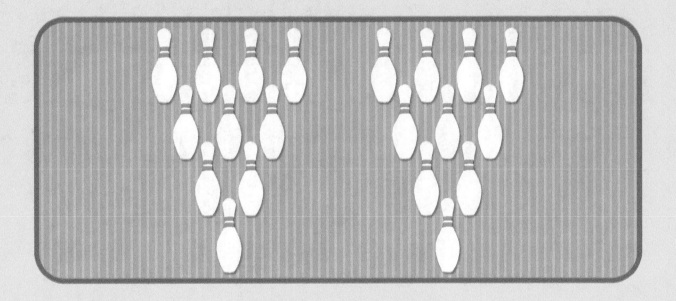

_____ groups of 10

_____ pins in all

Circle the groups of 10 pins in each set. Write how many groups of 10 you circled. Write how many pins in all.

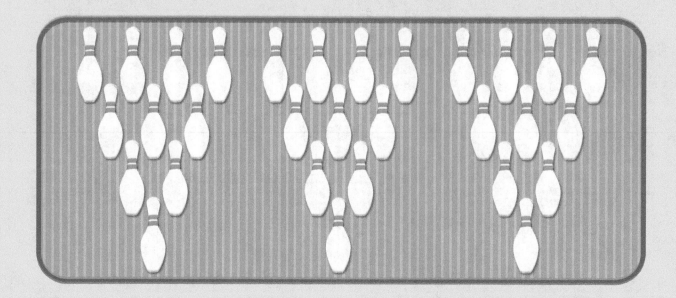

_____ groups of 10

_____ pins in all

Feeding Fun

Put 6 treats in the largest dish. Use counters. Divide the food so that each dog has the same amount.

Feeding Fun

Put 10 treats in the largest dish. Use counters. Divide the food so that each dog has the same amount.

Add the correct number of counters to each caterpillar to reach the sum. Write the numbers to show each part of the caterpillar.

_____ + _____ = 8 parts

_____ + _____ = 10 parts

_____ + _____ = 7 parts

Caterpillar Count

Add the correct number of counters to each caterpillar to reach the sum. Write the numbers to show each part of the caterpillar.

_____ + _____ = 5 parts

_____ + _____ = 9 parts

_____ + _____ = 6 parts

Roll 2 dice and put 1 die in each small box. Put counters in each large box to show each rolled number. Add the numbers for each set. Write the sum.

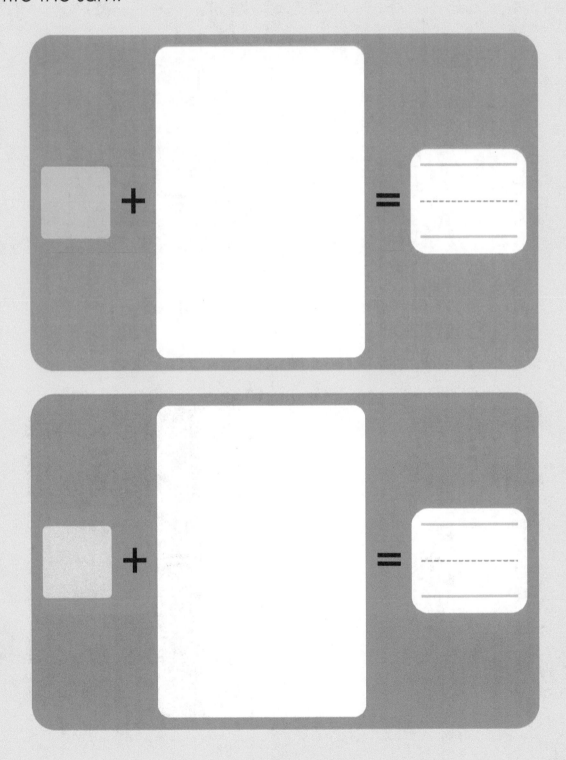

Roll 4 dice and put 2 dice in each small box. Put counters in each large box to show each rolled number. Add the numbers for each set. Write the sum.

Use two-color counters to show 3 ways to make 10 on the ten frame. Write the addition number sentences on the lines.

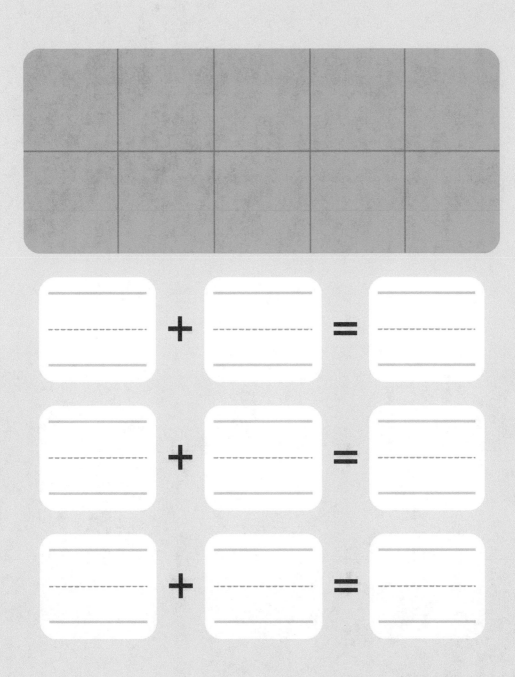

Make Ten

Use two-color counters to show 3 more ways to make 10 on the ten frame. Write the addition number sentences on the lines.

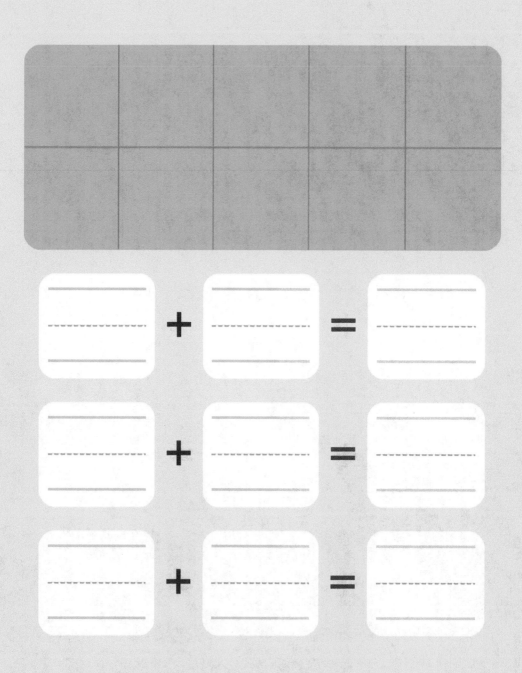

The kangaroo is hopping backward on each number line. Write the numbers to complete each sentence.

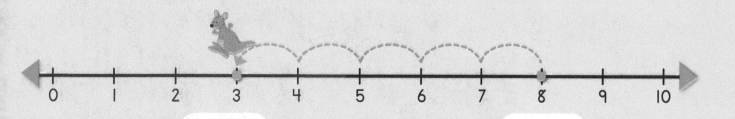

I started on _____ . I hopped back _____ spaces.

I landed on _____ .

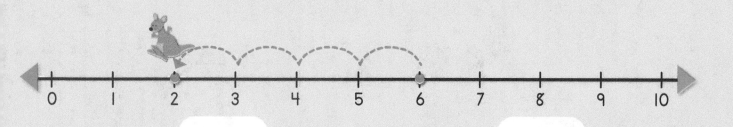

I started on _____ . I hopped back _____ spaces.

I landed on _____ .

The kangaroo is hopping backward on each number line. Write the numbers to complete each sentence.

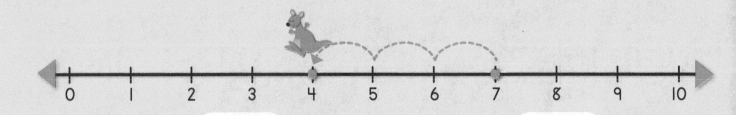

I started on _____. I hopped back _____ spaces.

I landed on _____.

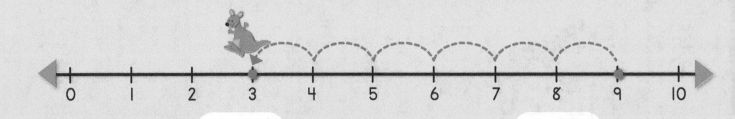

I started on _____. I hopped back _____ spaces.

I landed on _____.

Solve each word problem. Use counters to compare the number of objects each pair of whales can hold.

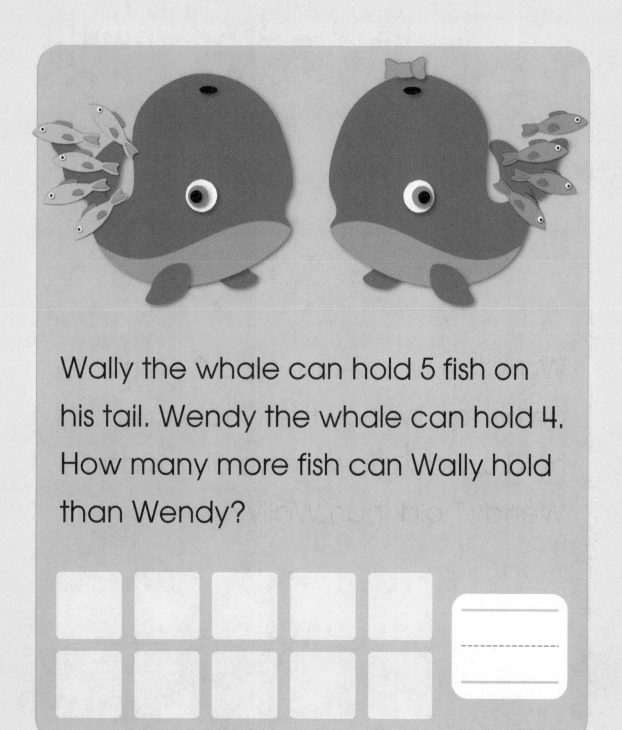

Wally the whale can hold 5 fish on his tail. Wendy the whale can hold 4. How many more fish can Wally hold than Wendy?

Solve each word problem. Use counters to compare the number of objects each pair of whales can hold.

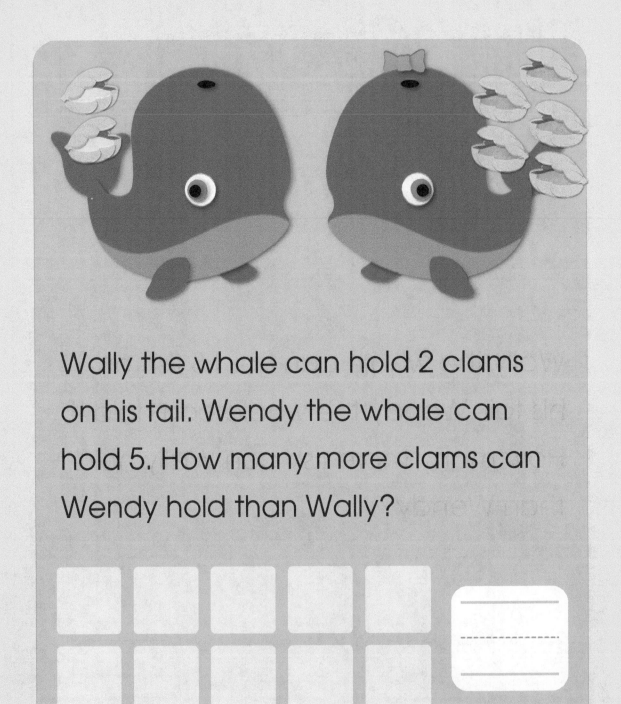

Wally the whale can hold 2 clams on his tail. Wendy the whale can hold 5. How many more clams can Wendy hold than Wally?

Put ice cream scoops on each cone to solve each problem.

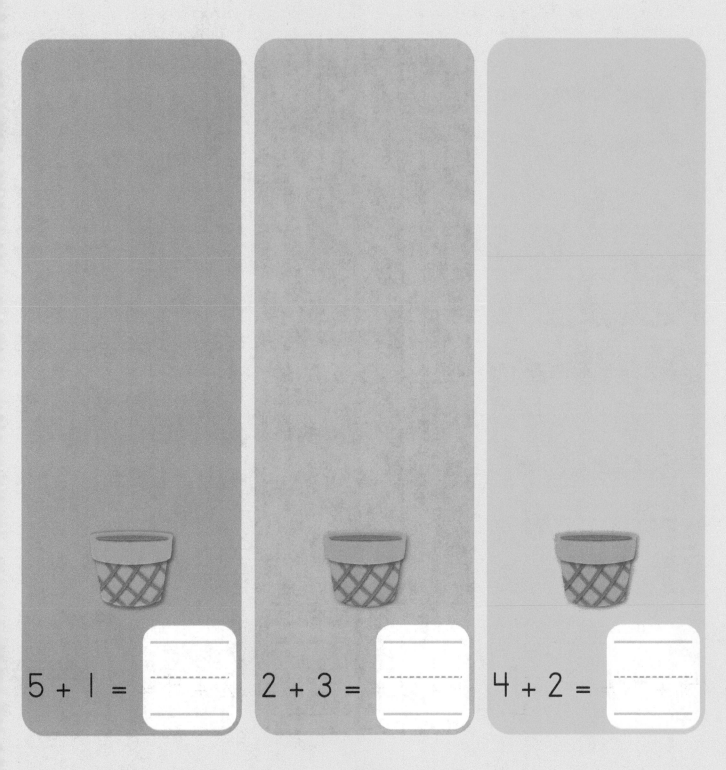

5 + 1 = _____

2 + 3 = _____

4 + 2 = _____

Put ice cream scoops on each cone to solve each problem.

4 + 1 = _____

1 + 3 = _____

2 + 4 = _____

Write the number sentence for each picture.

Too Many Toys!

Write the number sentence for each picture.

$$\boxed{} - \boxed{} = \boxed{}$$

$$\boxed{} - \boxed{} = \boxed{}$$

Look at each number sentence. Find each missing number by circling the food items that are left over.

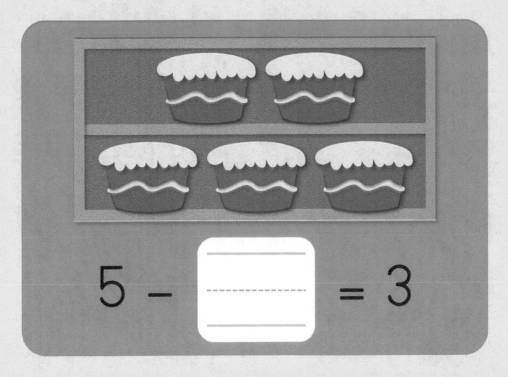

$$5 - \underline{} = 3$$

$$6 - \underline{} = 4$$

At the Bakery

Look at each number sentence. Find each missing number by circling the food items that are left over.

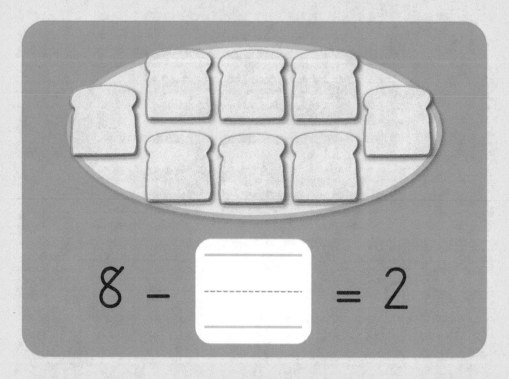

$$8 - \underline{} = 2$$

$$7 - \underline{} = 1$$

Write the number that each animal is hiding.

$2 + $ 🐘 $= 5$

🐘 $= $ _____

$7 - $ 🐯 $= 4$

🐯 $= $ _____

🐼 $- 5 = 2$

🐼 $= $ _____

© Carson-Dellosa
CD-704461

Move That Animal!

Write the number that each animal is hiding.

+ 3 = 6

🦁 = _____

1 + 🐵 = 3

🐵 = _____

9 − 🐧 = 8

🐧 = _____

Sporty Patterns

Use letters to name the first two patterns. Then, draw objects in the last row to show the letter pattern given.

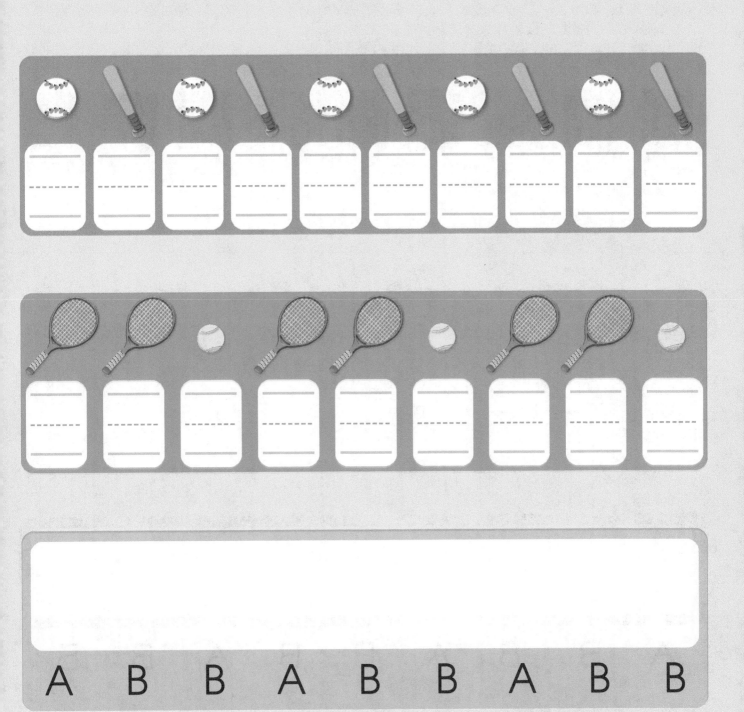

A B B A B B A B B

Use letters to name the first two patterns. Then, draw objects in the last row to show the letter pattern given.

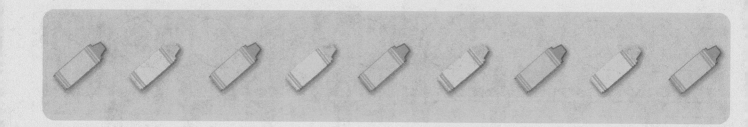

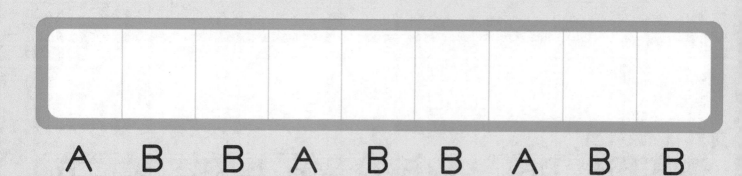

A B B A B B B A B B

Traffic Patterns

Look at each pattern of cars. Use counters or cubes to copy and extend each pattern.

Fish Tanks

Study each row of fish tanks. Draw fish to complete each pattern.

Name That Shape

Write the name of each shape. Circle the pictures in each box that are the same shape.

square   triangle

Name That Shape

Write the name of each shape. Circle the pictures in each box that are the same shape.

circle   rectangle

What Shape Is This?

Write the name of each shape. Find and trace two pattern blocks for each shape.

hexagon	rhombus	trapezoid

What Shape Is This?

Write the name of each shape. Find and trace two pattern blocks for each shape.

square	triangle	circle

Write the name of each figure. Circle the picture in each box that is the same figure.

cube   sphere

Write the name of each figure. Circle the picture in each box that is the same figure.

cone   cylinder

Look at the pattern on the container. Sort the shapes onto the correct container. Use blocks or counters.

Packing for the Beach

Look at the patterns on the containers. Sort the shapes onto the correct containers. Use blocks or counters.

Write the number of sides and corners in each dotted shape.

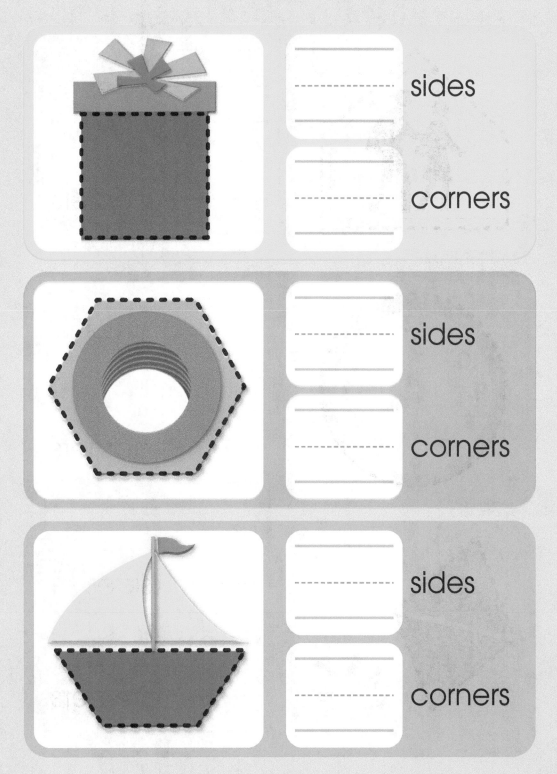

------------ sides

------------ corners

------------ sides

------------ corners

------------ sides

------------ corners

Write the number of sides and corners in each dotted shape.

_____ sides

_____ corners

_____ sides

_____ corners

_____ sides

_____ corners

Picture That Shape

Count the shapes in the picture. Write the total number of each shape.

_____ squares

_____ rhombuses

_____ hexagons

Picture That Shape

Count the shapes in the picture. Write the total number of each shape.

_____ triangles

_____ circles

Mystery Shapes

Estimate how many of each shape will fit inside the hexagon. Write the number. Use blocks to check each answer. Write the actual number.

Estimate	Actual

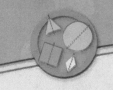

Hide-and-Seek

Look at the picture. Write the correct word or words to complete each sentence.

behind

beside

next to

on

under

The lamp is _____ the table.

The cat is _____ the table.

The girl is _____ the table.

The book is _____ the lamp.

The picture is _____ the girl.

Kitten Adventures

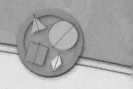

Help the kittens find the objects. Circle left or right and write how many spaces each kitten has to move to find her object.

		left right		spaces
	to	left right	_____	spaces
	to	left right	_____	spaces
	to	left right	_____	spaces
	to	left right	_____	spaces

Space Paces

Help the aliens find their homes. Circle up or down and write how many spaces each alien has to move to find his home.

to ☄ up down _____ spaces

to 🌙 up down _____ spaces

to 🪐 up down _____ spaces

to ☆ up down _____ spaces

Shape Symmetry

Circle the shape in each pair that has a correct line of symmetry.

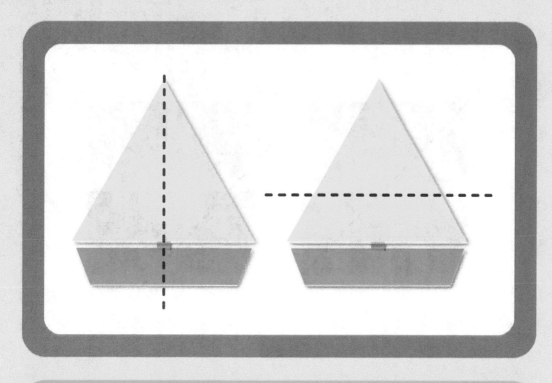

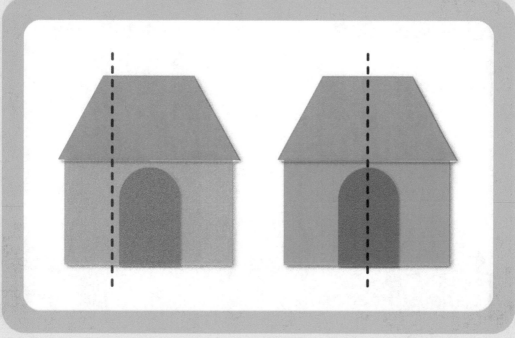

Shape Symmetry

Circle the shape in the pair that has a correct line of symmetry. In the last box, draw a picture with one line of symmetry.

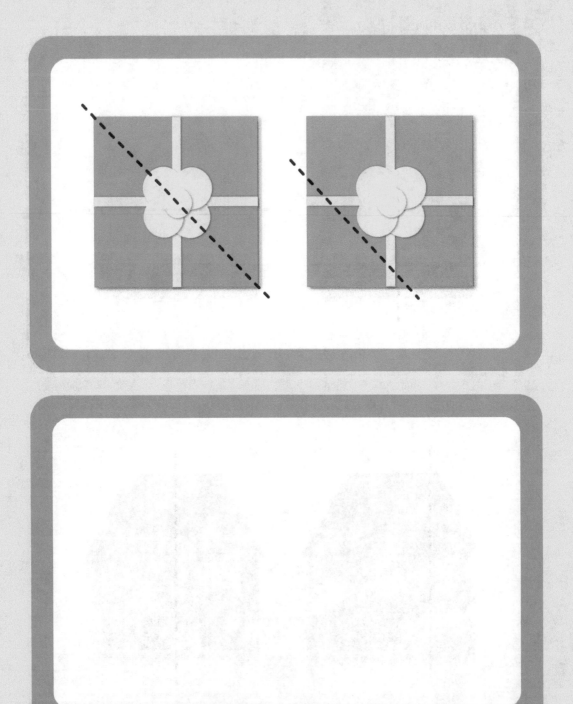

Letter Symmetry

Choose 6 letters and write them on the lines below. Sort each letter onto the correct side of the chalkboard.

Symmetry	No Symmetry

Letter Symmetry

Choose 6 more letters and write them on the lines below. Sort each letter onto the correct side of the chalkboard.

Symmetry	No Symmetry

Put a matching block on each shape.

Sort a handful of blocks by the number of corners.

0 corners	3 corners	4 corners

Count the number of each shape. Write the total number beside the correct name.

_____ triangles

_____ squares

_____ rectangles

_____ circles

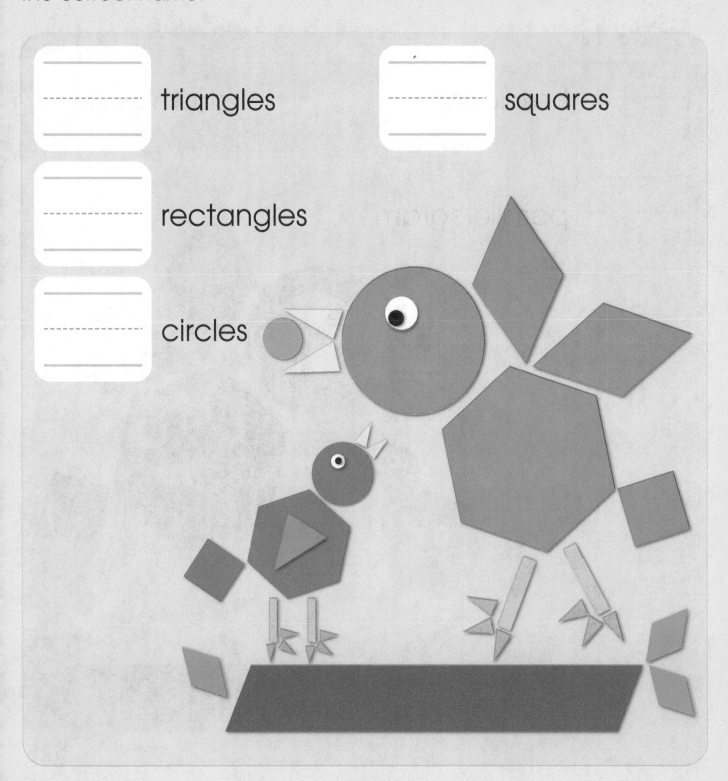

Count the number of each shape. Write the total number beside the correct name.

_____ hexagons

_____ rhombuses

_____ parallelogram

Soccer Practice

Use cubes or counters to measure each soccer player's path from the ball to the net. Circle the player who has the longest path.

Pandas and Bamboo

Write the numbers 1 to 5 to order the bamboo stalks from shortest to tallest.

Use cubes or counters to cover each leaf. Write how many cubes or counters it takes to cover each leaf.

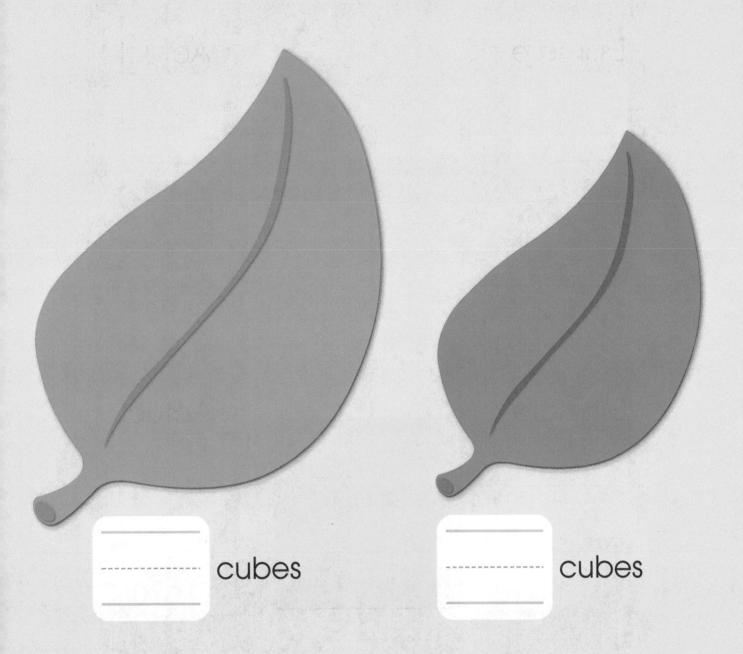

_____ cubes

_____ cubes

What's the Area?

Estimate how many counters it takes to cover each shape. Write the number. Then, cover each shape with counters. Write the actual number.

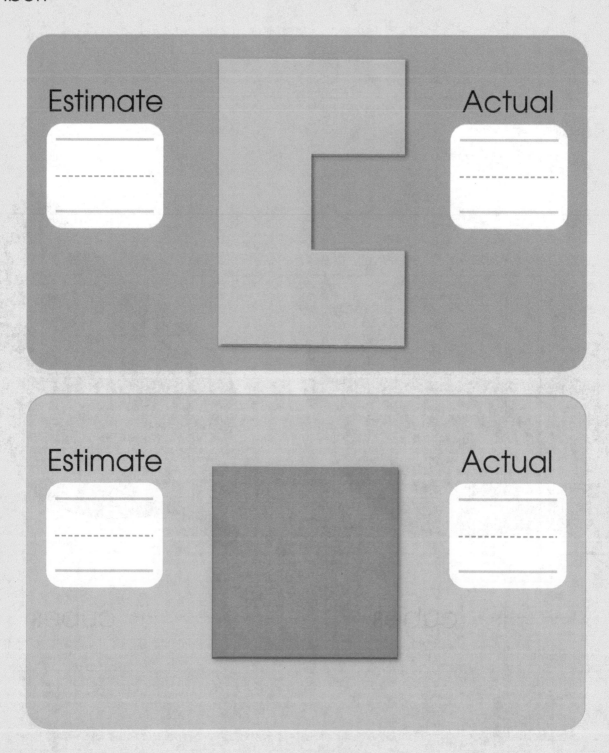

Estimate

Actual

Estimate

Actual

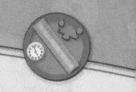

Estimate how many counters it takes to cover each shape. Write the number. Then, cover each shape with counters. Write the actual number.

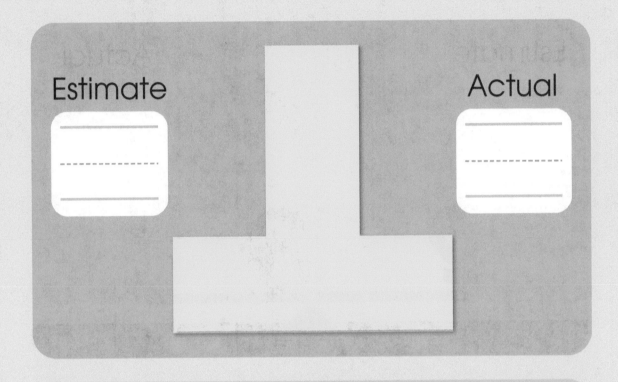

Estimate

Actual

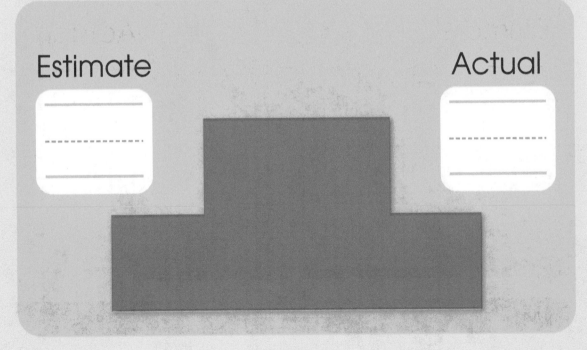

Estimate

Actual

Estimate how many counters each object weighs. Put the object on a scale. Put counters on the other side of the scale until it balances. Write how many counters it takes to balance the scale.

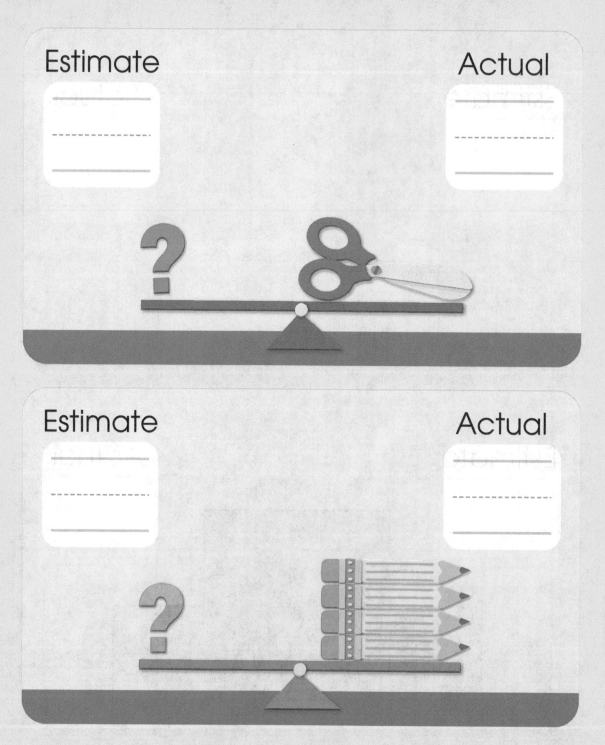

Estimate

Actual

Estimate

Actual

Estimate how many counters each object weighs. Put the object on a scale. Put counters on the other side of the scale until it balances. Write how many counters it takes to balance the scale.

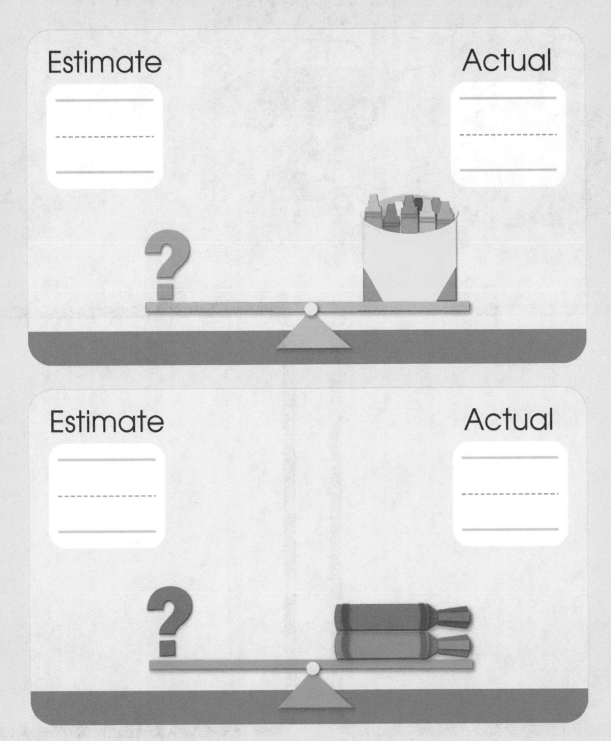

Estimate

Actual

Estimate

Actual

Heavy or Light?

Circle the object in each pair that is heavier. Draw two more pairs of objects and circle the objects that are heavier.

Use counters to measure each object. Write the number.

The polar bear is _____ counters long.

The fish is _____ counters long.

© Carson-Dellosa

Use counters to measure the object. Write the number.

The igloo is ▭ counters tall.

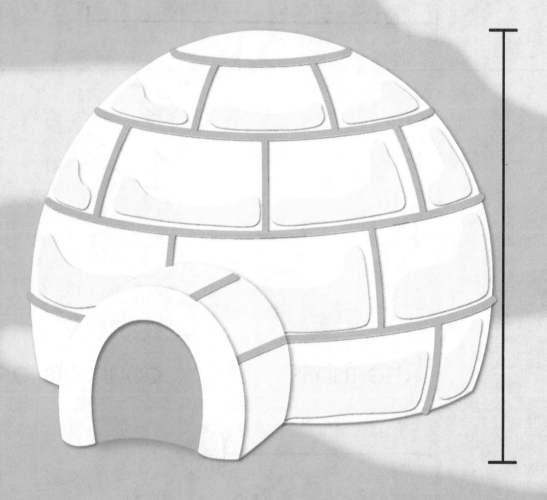

Use counters to measure each string. Write the number.

counters

counters

Use counters to measure each string. Write the number.

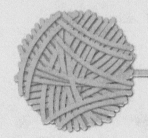

counters

counters

Snail Trails

Use counters to measure the snail's trail from vegetable to vegetable. Write the number.

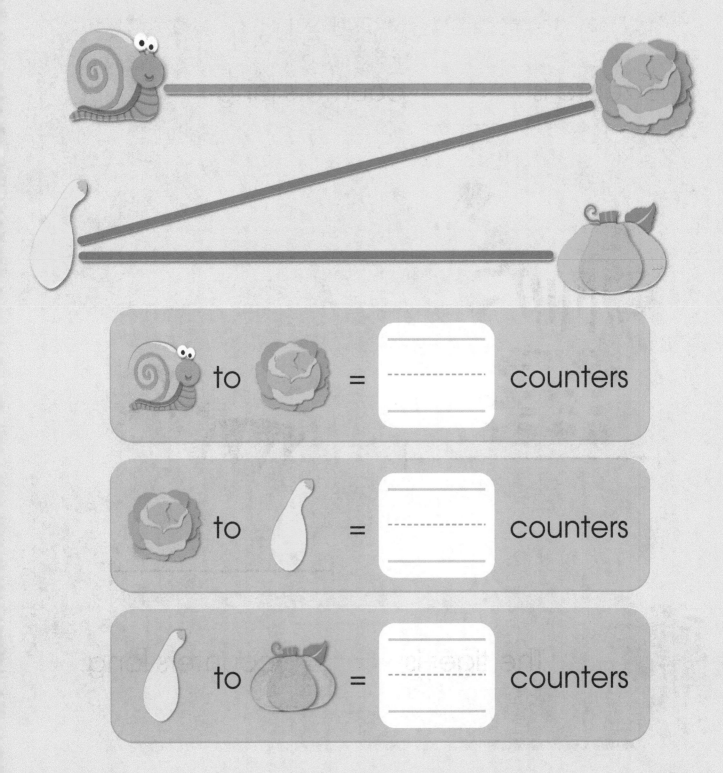

Use counters to measure each animal. Write the number.

The zebra is _____ counters long.

The tiger is _____ counters long.

Use counters to measure the animal. Write the number.

The giraffe is _____ counters tall.

Out of This World

Use a ruler to measure the spaceship's paths through space in centimeters. Write each number on the correct line.

🚀 to 🪐 = _____ cm   🌑 to ⭐ = _____ cm

🪐 to 🌑 = _____ cm   ⭐ to 🚀 = _____ cm

Use a ruler to measure each animal in inches. Write the number.

The starfish is _____ inches wide.

The crab is _____ inches wide.

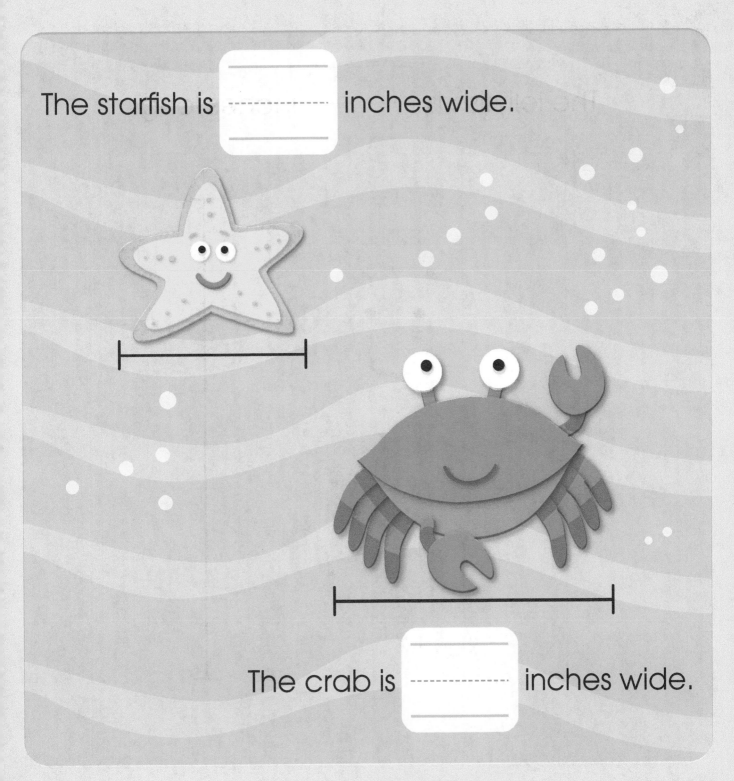

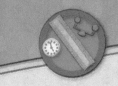

Use a ruler to measure the animal in inches. Write the number.

The jellyfish is _____ inches long.

Ready, Set, Go!

Use a ruler to measure each path around the track in inches. Write each number on the correct line.

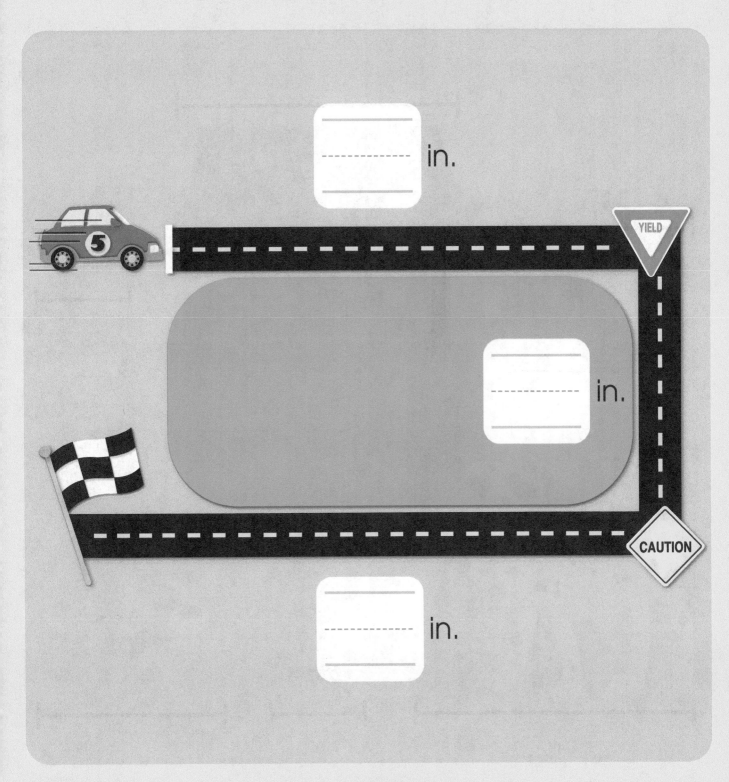

_____ in.

_____ in.

_____ in.

Doghouses

Measure each dog and doghouse in inches. Then, draw a line to connect each dog to the correct doghouse.

Put a button on each shirt that matches the color. Then, trace the color word.

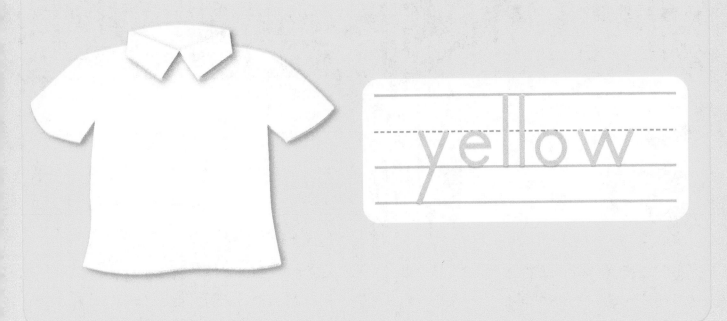

yellow

red

Put a button on each shirt that matches the color. Then, trace the color word.

blue

green

Put a button on each shirt that matches the color. Then, trace the color word.

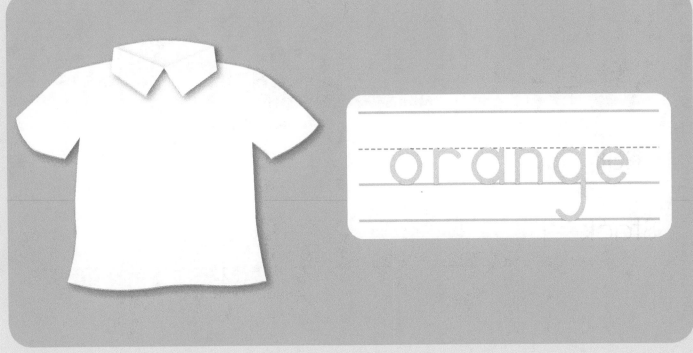

Roll or Stack?

Decide whether each figure will roll, stack, or do both. Circle each object that will roll. Draw an X on each object that will stack. Make a tally mark in the correct box or boxes.

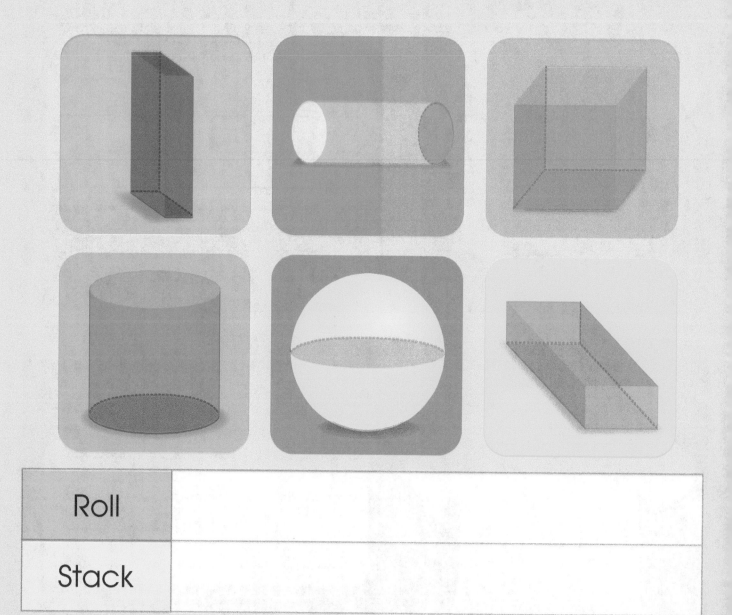

Roll	
Stack	

Write each letter in the correct space on the diagram.

X S A J O

Straight Lines

Both

Curvy Lines

Write each letter in the correct space on the diagram.

U G K E M

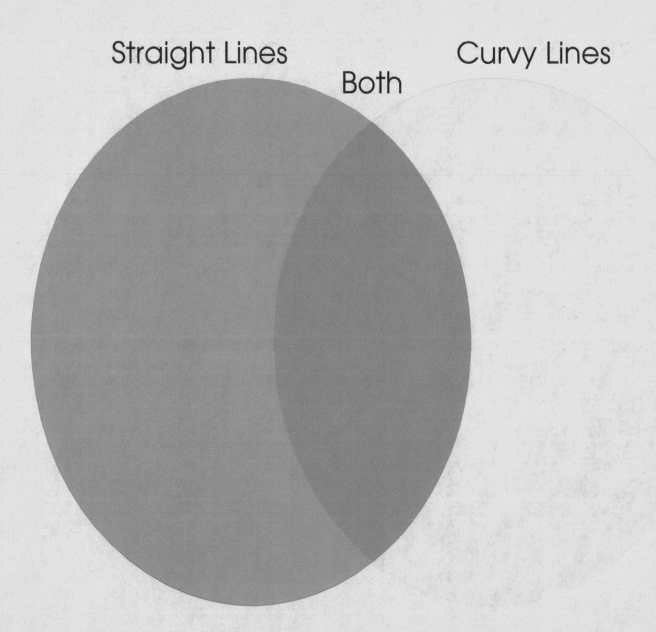

Straight Lines   Curvy Lines

Both

Write each letter in the correct space on the diagram.

Q W C Z B

Straight Lines   **Curvy Lines**

Both

Butterfly Garden

Put matching colored buttons on each butterfly. Then, move the buttons onto the bar graph to graph the data.

Look at the graph. Write how many of each animal is at the zoo.

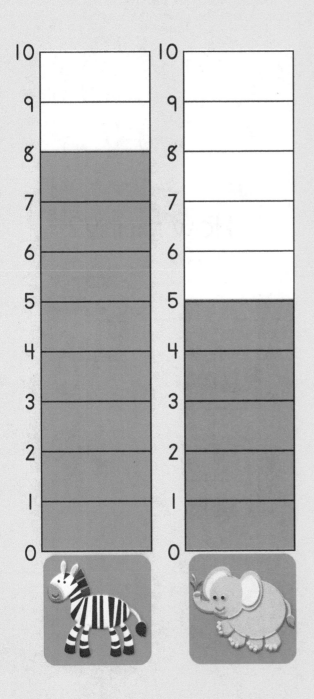

How many?

Look at the graph. Write how many of each animal is at the zoo.

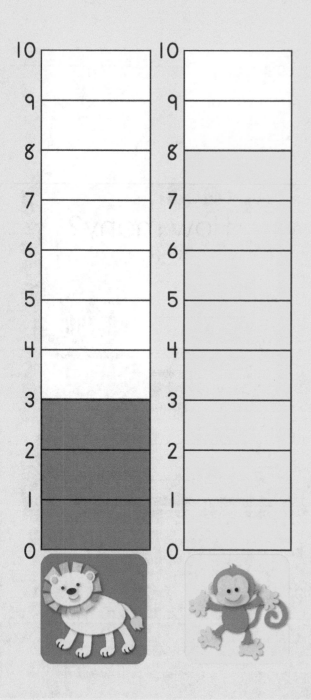

How many?

Put the correct color of button on each animal. Then, graph the information and write tally marks for each animals's total.

Fruit Trees

Count the fruit on each tree. Use cubes to graph the total number of each fruit. Then, write tally marks for each fruit's total.

Put the correct color of button on each type of weather. Make a tally chart to show the information.

Sunday	Monday	Tuesday	Wednesday	Thursday	Friday	Saturday
					☀	☀
☀	☀	☀	🌧	☁	☀	☀
☀	🌧	🌧	☁	☀	☀	☀
🌧	☁	☀	☀	☀	☁	🌧
☀	☀	☁	☀	🌧	🌧	☁
☀						

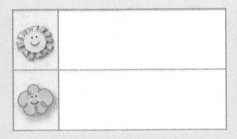

5

6

7

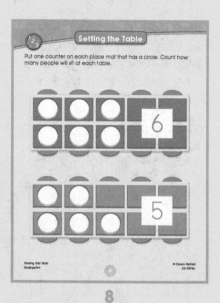

8

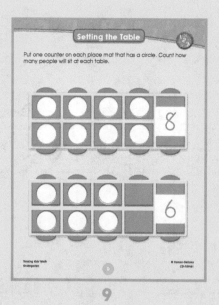

9

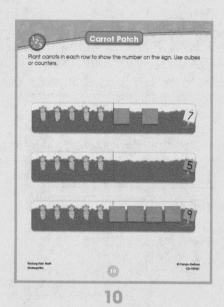

10

Answer Key

Carrot Patch

Plant carrots in each row to show the number on the sign. Use cubes or counters.

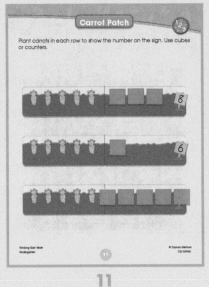

8

6

Thinking Kids' Math
Kindergarten
11
© Carson-Dellosa
CD-704461

11

On the Farm

Put 10 sheep in the barn. Use counters. Put the rest outside of the barn. Count how many are outside.

11

1 sheep

Thinking Kids' Math
Kindergarten
12
© Carson-Dellosa
CD-704461

12

On the Farm

Put 10 horses in the barn. Use counters. Put the rest outside of the barn. Count how many are outside.

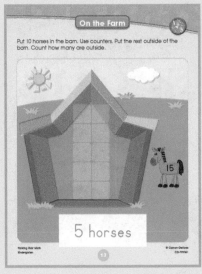

15

5 horses

Thinking Kids' Math
Kindergarten
13
© Carson-Dellosa
CD-704461

13

On the Farm

Put 10 cows in the barn. Use counters. Put the rest outside of the barn. Count how many are outside.

17

7 cows

Thinking Kids' Math
Kindergarten
14
© Carson-Dellosa
CD-704461

14

On the Farm

Put 10 sheep in the barn. Use counters. Put the rest outside of the barn. Count how many are outside.

13

3 sheep

Thinking Kids' Math
Kindergarten
15
© Carson-Dellosa
CD-704461

15

Apple Picking

Take a handful of apples and put them on the tree. Use counters. Move the apples to the ten frames. Count how many total apples.

Answers will vary.

Thinking Kids' Math
Kindergarten
16
© Carson-Dellosa
CD-704461

16

Answer Key

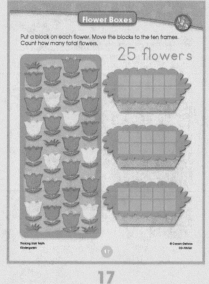

Flower Boxes

Put a block on each flower. Move the blocks to the ten frames.
Count how many total flowers.

25 flowers

17

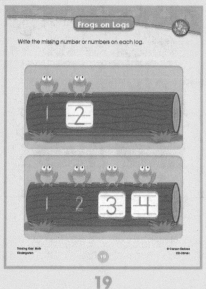

Ducks in a Pond

Put a block on each duck. Move the blocks to the ten frames.
Count how many total ducks.

30 ducks

18

Frogs on Logs

Write the missing number or numbers on each log.

1 **2**

1 2 **3 4**

19

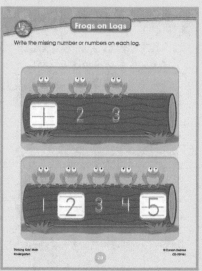

Frogs on Logs

Write the missing number or numbers on each log.

1 2 3

1 2 3 4 **5**

20

Frogs on Logs

Write the missing number or numbers on each log.

1 **2** 3 **4**

1 2 3 **4**

21

Frogs on Logs

Write the missing number or numbers on each log.

1 2 **3**

1 **2 3** 4 **5**

22

23

24

25

26

Ordinal Trains

Put one matching colored cube on each train car. Then, answer the questions.

What color is each car?

1st	black
3rd	brown
6th	green
8th	orange

27

Ordinal Trains

Put one matching colored cube on each train car. Then, answer the questions.

What color is each car?

2nd	white
4th	blue
5th	light blue
9th	red

28

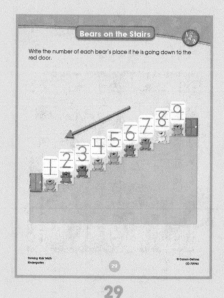

29

30

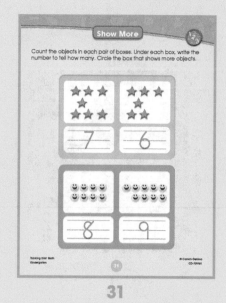

31

32

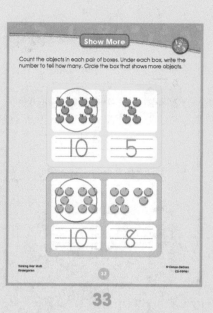

33

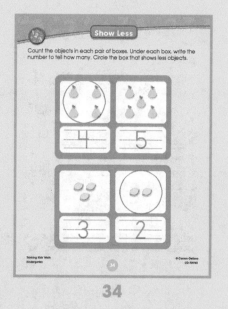

34

Full of Fish

Put 10 fish in the first fish tank. Use counters. Put 7 fish in the second fish tank. Write each number. Then, circle more or less.

10

more **7** (less)

Full of Fish

Put a handful of fish in the first fish tank. Use counters. Put more or less fish in the second fish tank. Write each number. Then, circle more or less.

Answers will vary.

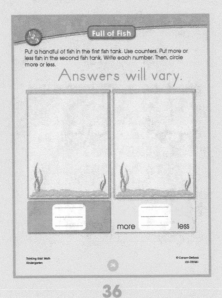

more ___ less

More Spots

Circle the dog in each pair that has more spots.

35

36

37

Less Spots

Circle the dog in each pair that has less spots.

Nest Egg

Roll a die. Put that number of eggs in the middle nest. Use counters. Put less eggs in the first nest and more eggs in the last nest. Write each number.

Answers will vary.

eggs eggs eggs

less   more

Ladybug Spots

Count the spots on each ladybug. Write the number.

4

7

38

39

40

Answer Key

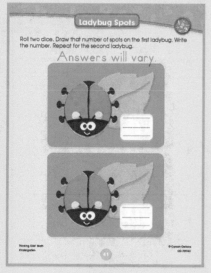

Ladybug Spots

Roll two dice. Draw that number of spots on the first ladybug. Write the number. Repeat for the second ladybug.

Answers will vary.

Thinking Kids' Math
Kindergarten

© Carson-Dellosa
CD-704461

41

Ladybug Spots

Roll two dice. Draw that number of spots on the first ladybug. Write the number. Use counters to show different ways to make that same number on the other ladybugs. Draw the spots.

Answers will vary.

Thinking Kids' Math
Kindergarten

© Carson-Dellosa
CD-704461

42

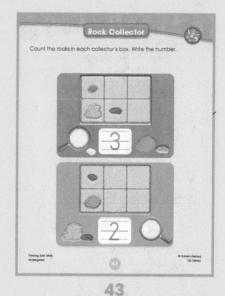

Rock Collector

Count the rocks in each collector's box. Write the number.

3

2

Thinking Kids' Math
Kindergarten

© Carson-Dellosa
CD-704461

43

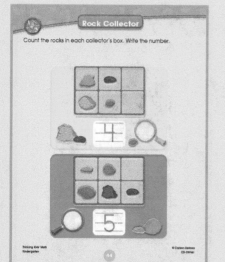

Rock Collector

Count the rocks in each collector's box. Write the number.

4

5

Thinking Kids' Math
Kindergarten

© Carson-Dellosa
CD-704461

44

Rock Collector

Roll the die. Put that number of rocks in the first collector's box. Write the number. Repeat for the other collector's box.

Answers will vary.

Thinking Kids' Math
Kindergarten

© Carson-Dellosa
CD-704461

45

Cookie Jar

Count the cookies. Write the number. Put that number of counters in the ten frame.

8

Thinking Kids' Math
Kindergarten

© Carson-Dellosa
CD-704461

46

Answer Key

Cookie Jar

Drop 10 cookies onto the jar. Use counters. Move the cookies that land on the jar to the ten frame. Count the cookies and write the number.

10

47

How Many Crackers?

Count the crackers on the plate. Write the number and the number word.

5   five

48

How Many Crackers?

Roll 3 dice. Count that many crackers and put them on the plate. Use counters. Move the crackers to the ten frames. Write the number and the number word.

Answers will vary.

49

Same or Different?

Count the objects in each pair of boxes. Under each box, write the number to tell how many. Circle same or different.

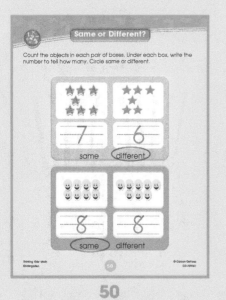

7   6
same   (different)

8   8
(same)   different

50

Same or Different?

Count the objects in each pair of boxes. Under each box, write the number to tell how many. Circle same or different.

9   10
same   (different)

6   6
(same)   different

51

Fair Shares

Look at each pair of foods. Circle the food in each pair that shows equal parts.

52

Answer Key

Fair Shares
53

Circle the sandwich that shows equal parts. In the second box, draw a line on the cracker to show equal parts.

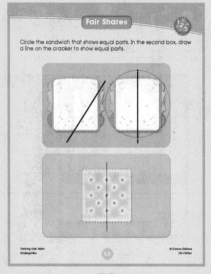

Apple Tree Addition
54

Put counters on the apples in each tree. Count the apples. Write how many apples in all.

$+$ $=$ 5

$+$ $=$ 4

Apple Tree Addition
55

Put counters on the apples in each tree. Count the apples. Write how many apples in all.

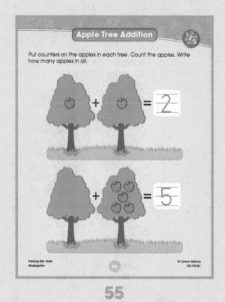

$+$ $=$ 2

$+$ $=$ 5

Domino Addition
56

Put a domino in each box. Count the dots on each half of the domino. Write the numbers on the lines. Add the numbers and write the sum.

Answers will vary.

$+$ $=$

$+$ $=$

Domino Addition
57

Put a domino in each box. Count the dots on each half of the domino. Write the numbers on the lines. Add the numbers and write the sum.

Answers will vary.

$+$ $=$

$+$ $=$

Number Popping
58

Put 10 pieces of popcorn on the first bag. Roll a die and move that number of pieces from the first bag to the second bag. Write the number sentence to show how many pieces are left. Repeat 3 times.

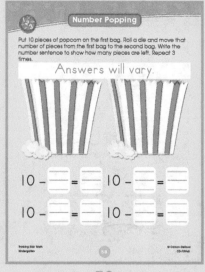

Answers will vary.

$10 -$ $=$ $10 -$ $=$

$10 -$ $=$ $10 -$ $=$

Number Popping

Put 15 pieces of popcorn on the first bag. Roll a die and move that number of pieces from the first bag to the second bag. Write the number sentence to show how many pieces are left. Repeat 3 times.

Answers will vary.

15 − ___ = ___   15 − ___ = ___

15 − ___ = ___   15 − ___ = ___

59

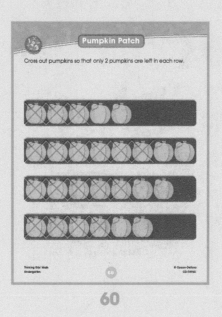

Pumpkin Patch

Cross out pumpkins so that only 2 pumpkins are left in each row.

60

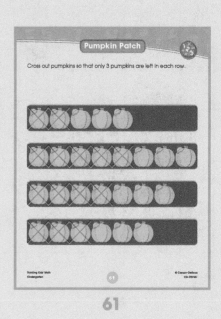

Pumpkin Patch

Cross out pumpkins so that only 3 pumpkins are left in each row.

61

Acro-bots

Use two colors of cubes to show a sum of 4. Write the number sentence. Flip the stack and write the new number sentence.

Answers will vary.

___ + ___ = ___

___ + ___ = ___

62

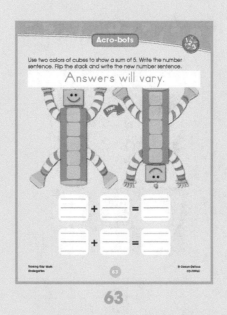

Acro-bots

Use two colors of cubes to show a sum of 5. Write the number sentence. Flip the stack and write the new number sentence.

Answers will vary.

___ + ___ = ___

___ + ___ = ___

63

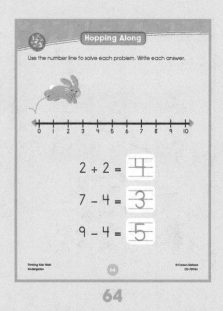

Hopping Along

Use the number line to solve each problem. Write each answer.

$2 + 2 = 4$

$7 − 4 = 3$

$9 − 4 = 5$

64

Answer Key

Hopping Along

Use the number line to solve each problem. Write each answer.

$1 + 7 = 8$

$8 - 2 = 6$

$10 - 3 = 7$

65

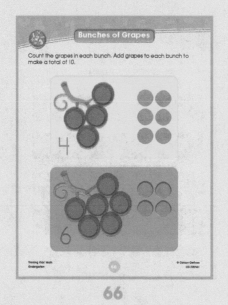

Bunches of Grapes

Count the grapes in each bunch. Add grapes to each bunch to make a total of 10.

4

6

66

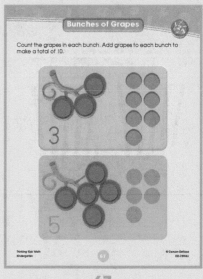

Bunches of Grapes

Count the grapes in each bunch. Add grapes to each bunch to make a total of 10.

3

5

67

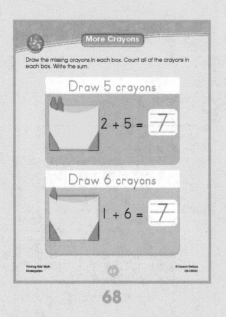

More Crayons

Draw the missing crayons in each box. Count all of the crayons in each box. Write the sum.

Draw 5 crayons

$2 + 5 = 7$

Draw 6 crayons

$1 + 6 = 7$

68

More Crayons

Draw the missing crayons in each box. Count all of the crayons in each box. Write the sum.

Draw 2 crayons

$5 + 2 = 7$

Draw 3 crayons

$4 + 3 = 7$

69

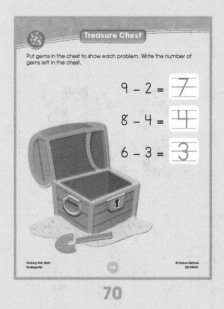

Treasure Chest

Put gems in the chest to show each problem. Write the number of gems left in the chest.

$9 - 2 = 7$

$8 - 4 = 4$

$6 - 3 = 3$

70

Thinking Kids™ Math

Kindergarten

176

© Carson-Dellosa

CD-704461

Answer Key

71

Treasure Chest

Put gems in the chest to show each problem. Write the number of gems left in the chest.

$7 - 2 = 5$

$8 - 2 = 6$

$9 - 8 = 1$

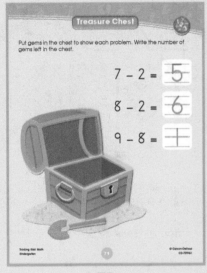

71

72

Squirrel Subtraction

Each squirrel ate some acorns. Cross out the number of acorns that each squirrel ate. Write how many acorns are left.

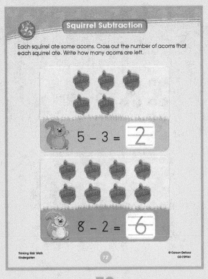

$5 - 3 = 2$

$8 - 2 = 6$

72

73

Squirrel Subtraction

Each squirrel ate some acorns. Cross out the number of acorns that each squirrel ate. Write how many acorns are left.

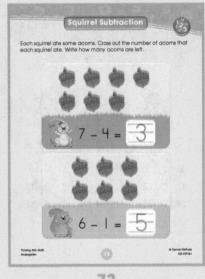

$7 - 4 = 3$

$6 - 1 = 5$

73

74

Mitten Count

Count by 2s. Write the numbers. Then, circle the numbers on the chart that you counted.

2 4 6 8 10

12 14 16 18 20

1 2 3 4 5 6 7 8 9 10
11 12 13 14 15 16 17 18 19 20

74

75

Pairs of Shoes

Circle each pair of shoes. Then, answer the questions.

How many children? 5

How many shoes? 10

75

76

Pairs of Shoes

Circle each pair of shoes. Then, answer the questions.

How many children? 8

How many shoes? 16

76

Answer Key

Give Me Five!

Count by 5s. Write the numbers. Then, circle the numbers on the chart that you counted.

5 10 15 20 25 30

1	2	3	4	⑤	6	7	8	9	⑩
11	12	13	14	⑮	16	17	18	19	⑳
21	22	23	24	㉕	26	27	28	29	㉚

77

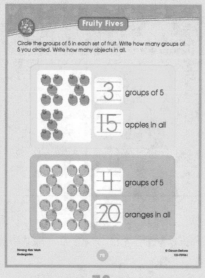

Fruity Fives

Circle the groups of 5 in each set of fruit. Write how many groups of 5 you circled. Write how many objects in all.

3 groups of 5
15 apples in all

4 groups of 5
20 oranges in all

78

Fruity Fives

Circle the groups of 5 in each set of fruit. Write how many groups of 5 you circled. Write how many objects in all.

2 groups of 5
10 pears in all

1 groups of 5
5 lemons in all

79

Let's Count Tens

Count by 10s. Write the numbers. Then, circle the numbers on the chart that you counted.

10 20 30 40 50

1	2	3	4	5	6	7	8	9	⑩
11	12	13	14	15	16	17	18	19	⑳
21	22	23	24	25	26	27	28	29	㉚
31	32	33	34	35	36	37	38	39	㊵
41	42	43	44	45	46	47	48	49	㊿

80

Let's Count to 100

Complete the chart by counting to 100.

1	2	3	4	5	6	7	8	9	10
11	12	13	14	15	16	17	18	19	20
21	22	23	24	25	26	27	28	29	30
31	32	33	34	35	36	37	38	39	40
41	42	43	44	45	46	47	48	49	50
51	52	53	54	55	56	57	58	59	60
61	62	63	64	65	66	67	68	69	70
71	72	73	74	75	76	77	78	79	80
81	82	83	84	85	86	87	88	89	90
91	92	93	94	95	96	97	98	99	100

81

Let's Count to 100

Complete the chart by counting to 100.

1	2	3	4	5	6	7	8	9	10
11	12	13	14	15	16	17	18	19	20
21	22	23	24	25	26	27	28	29	30
31	32	33	34	35	36	37	38	39	40
41	42	43	44	45	46	47	48	49	50
51	52	53	54	55	56	57	58	59	60
61	62	63	64	65	66	67	68	69	70
71	72	73	74	75	76	77	78	79	80
81	82	83	84	85	86	87	88	89	90
91	92	93	94	95	96	97	98	99	100

82

Ten Pins

Circle the groups of 10 pins in each set. Write how many groups of 10 you circled. Write how many pins in all.

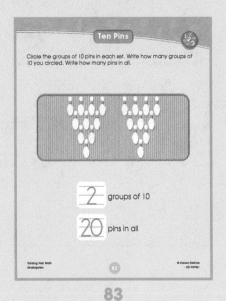

2 groups of 10

20 pins in all

Ten Pins

Circle the groups of 10 pins in each set. Write how many groups of 10 you circled. Write how many pins in all.

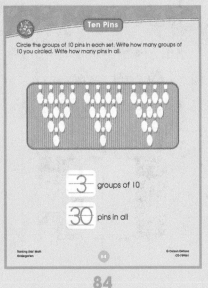

3 groups of 10

30 pins in all

Feeding Fun

Put 6 treats in the largest dish. Use counters. Divide the food so that each dog has the same amount.

Feeding Fun

Put 10 treats in the largest dish. Use counters. Divide the food so that each dog has the same amount.

Caterpillar Count

Add the correct number of counters to each caterpillar to reach the sum. Write the numbers to show each part of the caterpillar.

$3 + 5 = 8$ parts

$5 + 5 = 10$ parts

$4 + 3 = 7$ parts

Caterpillar Count

Add the correct number of counters to each caterpillar to reach the sum. Write the numbers to show each part of the caterpillar.

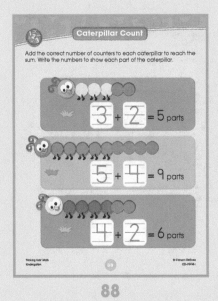

$3 + 2 = 5$ parts

$5 + 4 = 9$ parts

$4 + 2 = 6$ parts

Doubles

Roll 2 dice and put 1 die in each small box. Put counters in each large box to show each rolled number. Add the numbers for each set. Write the sum.

Answers will vary.

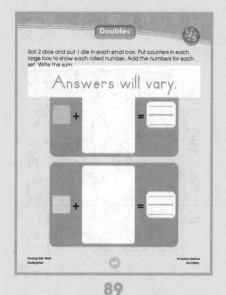

89

Doubles

Roll 4 dice and put 2 dice in each small box. Put counters in each large box to show each rolled number. Add the numbers for each set. Write the sum.

Answers will vary.

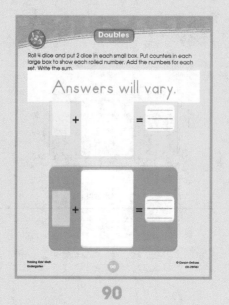

90

Make Ten

Use two-color counters to show 3 ways to make 10 on the ten frame. Write the addition number sentences on the lines.

Answers will vary.

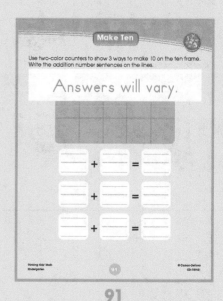

91

Make Ten

Use two-color counters to show 3 more ways to make 10 on the ten frame. Write the addition number sentences on the lines.

Answers will vary.

92

Kangaroo Hop

The kangaroo is hopping backward on each number line. Write the numbers to complete each sentence.

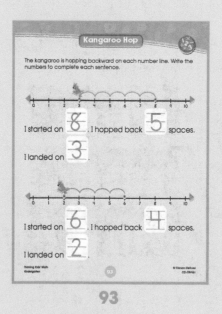

I started on **8**. I hopped back **5** spaces.

I landed on **3**.

I started on **6**. I hopped back **4** spaces.

I landed on **2**.

93

Kangaroo Hop

The kangaroo is hopping backward on each number line. Write the numbers to complete each sentence.

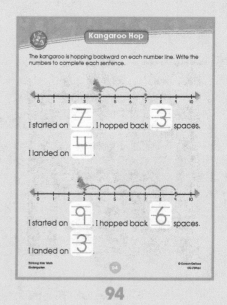

I started on **7**. I hopped back **3** spaces.

I landed on **4**.

I started on **9**. I hopped back **6** spaces.

I landed on **3**.

94

© Carson-Dellosa
CD-704461

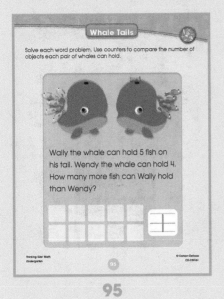

95

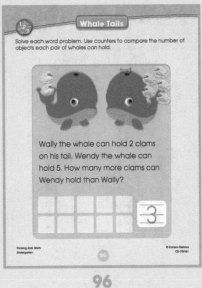

96

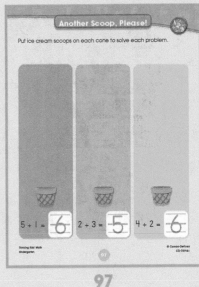

97

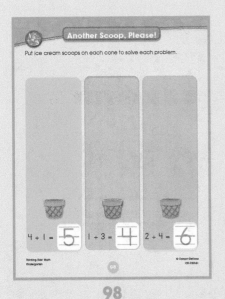

98

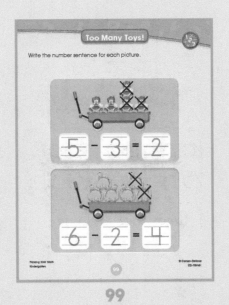

99

100

Answer Key

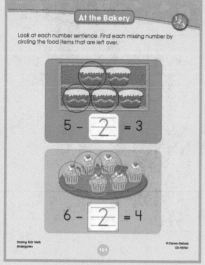

At the Bakery

Look at each number sentence. Find each missing number by circling the food items that are left over.

$5 - 2 = 3$

$6 - 2 = 4$

101

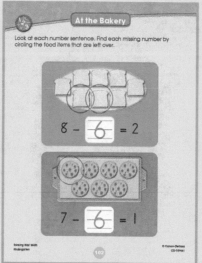

At the Bakery

Look at each number sentence. Find each missing number by circling the food items that are left over.

$8 - 6 = 2$

$7 - 6 = 1$

102

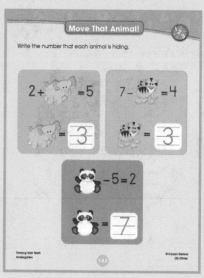

Move That Animal!

Write the number that each animal is hiding.

$2 + 3 = 5$

$3 = 3$

$7 - 3 = 4$

$3 = 3$

$-5 = 2$

$= 7$

103

Move That Animal!

Write the number that each animal is hiding.

$+ 3 = 6$

$= 3$

$1 + 2 = 3$

$= 2$

$9 - 1 = 8$

$= 1$

104

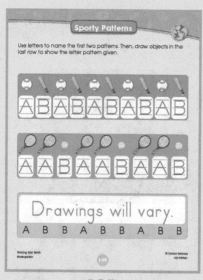

Sporty Patterns

Use letters to name the first two patterns. Then, draw objects in the last row to show the letter pattern given.

A B A B A B A B A B

A A B A A B A A B

Drawings will vary.

A B B A B B A B B

105

Matching Patterns

Use letters to name the first two patterns. Then, draw objects in the last row to show the letter pattern given.

A A B A A B A A B

A B A B A B A B A

Drawings will vary.

A B B A B B A B B

106

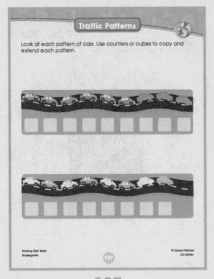

107

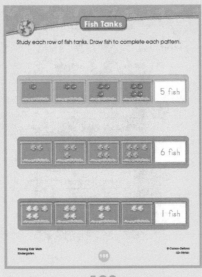

108

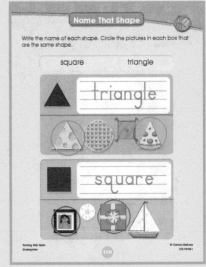

109

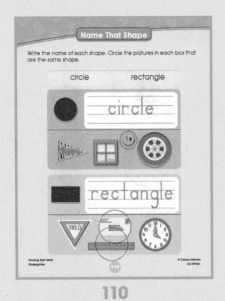

110

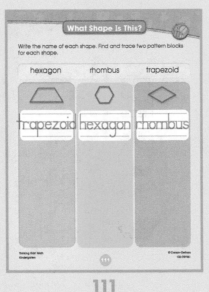

111

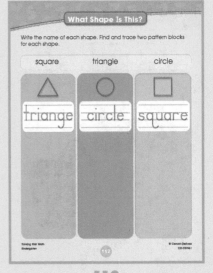

112

Answer Key

113

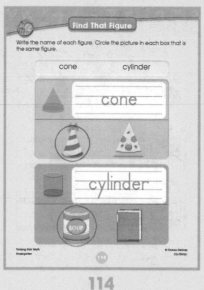

114

115

116

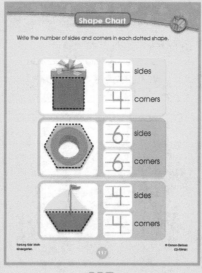

117

118

Picture That Shape

Count the shapes in the picture. Write the total number of each shape.

5 squares

3 rhombuses

2 hexagons

119

Picture That Shape

Count the shapes in the picture. Write the total number of each shape.

8 triangles

8 circles

120

Mystery Shapes

Estimate how many of each shape will fit inside the hexagon. Write the number. Use blocks to check each answer. Write the actual number.

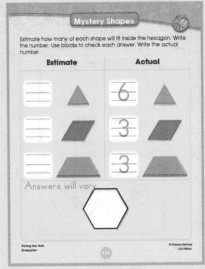

Estimate	Actual
	6
	3
	3

Answers will vary

121

Hide-and-Seek

Look at the picture. Write the correct word or words to complete each sentence.

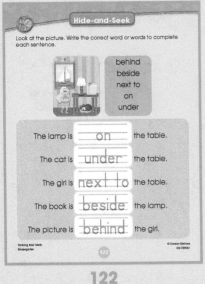

behind
beside
next to
on
under

The lamp is **on** the table.

The cat is **under** the table.

The girl is **next to** the table.

The book is **beside** the lamp.

The picture is **behind** the girl.

122

Kitten Adventures

Help the kittens find the objects. Circle left or right and write how many spaces each kitten has to move to find her object.

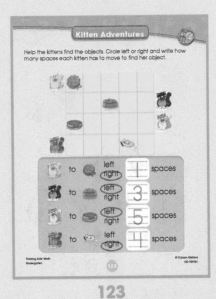

to (left) / right **4** spaces

to (left) / right **3** spaces

to left / (right) **5** spaces

to left / (right) **4** spaces

123

Space Paces

Help the aliens find their homes. Circle up or down and write how many spaces each alien has to move to find his home.

to up / (down) **3** spaces

to (up) / down **3** spaces

to up / (down) **2** spaces

to (up) / down **4** spaces

124

Answer Key

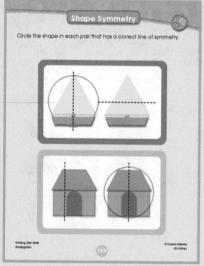

125

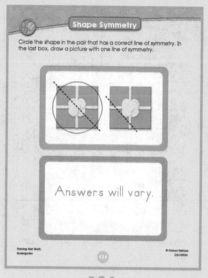

126

127

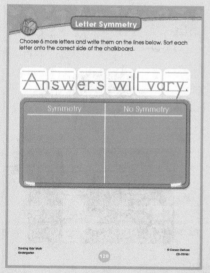

128

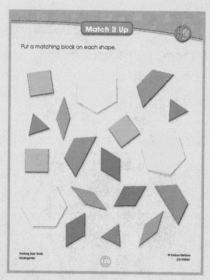

129

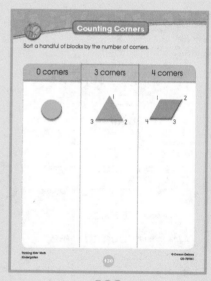

130

Answer Key

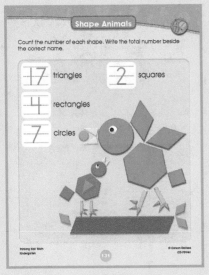

Shape Animals

Count the number of each shape. Write the total number beside the correct name.

17 triangles   2 squares
4 rectangles
7 circles

131

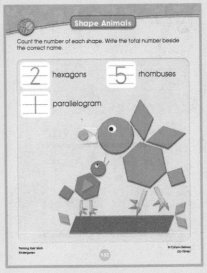

Shape Animals

Count the number of each shape. Write the total number beside the correct name.

2 hexagons   5 rhombuses
1 parallelogram

132

Soccer Practice

Use cubes or counters to measure each soccer player's path from the ball to the net. Circle the player who has the longest path.

133

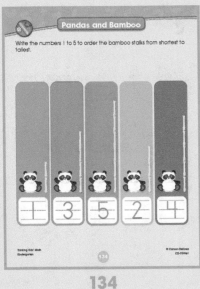

Pandas and Bamboo

Write the numbers 1 to 5 to order the bamboo stalks from shortest to tallest.

1   3   5   2   4

134

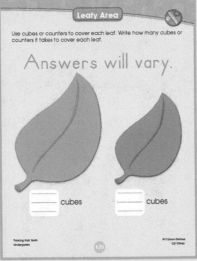

Leafy Area

Use cubes or counters to cover each leaf. Write how many cubes or counters it takes to cover each leaf.

Answers will vary.

____ cubes   ____ cubes

135

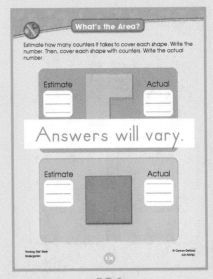

What's the Area?

Estimate how many counters it takes to cover each shape. Write the number. Then, cover each shape with counters. Write the actual number.

Estimate   Actual

Answers will vary.

Estimate   Actual

136

Thinking Kids™ Math
Kindergarten

187

© Carson-Dellosa
CD-704461

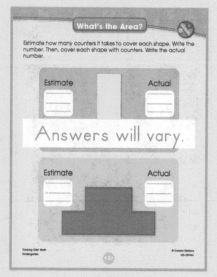

What's the Area?

Estimate how many counters it takes to cover each shape. Write the number. Then, cover each shape with counters. Write the actual number.

Estimate | Actual

Answers will vary.

Estimate | Actual

137

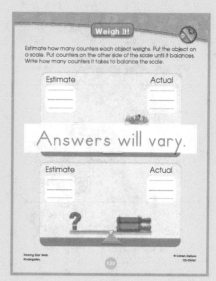

Weigh It!

Estimate how many counters each object weighs. Put the object on a scale. Put counters on the other side of the scale until it balances. Write how many counters it takes to balance the scale.

Estimate | Actual

Answers will vary.

Estimate | Actual

138

Weigh It!

Estimate how many counters each object weighs. Put the object on a scale. Put counters on the other side of the scale until it balances. Write how many counters it takes to balance the scale.

Estimate | Actual

Answers will vary.

Estimate | Actual

139

Heavy or Light?

Circle the object in each pair that is heavier. Draw two more pairs of objects and circle the objects that are heavier.

Drawings will vary.

140

Polar Measures

Use counters to measure each object. Write the number.

Answers will vary.

The polar bear is _____ counters long.

The fish is _____ counters long.

141

Polar Measures

Use counters to measure the object. Write the number.

Answers will vary.

The igloo is _____ counters tall.

142

Answer Key

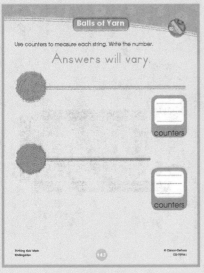

143

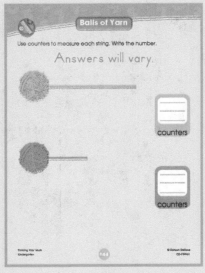

144

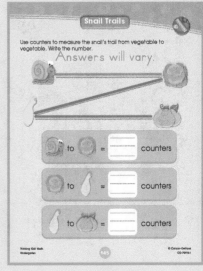

145

146

147

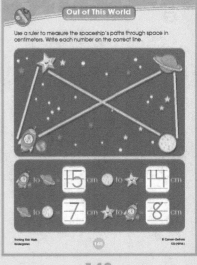

148

Answer Key

Sea Friends

Use a ruler to measure each animal in inches. Write the number.

The starfish is **2** inches wide.

The crab is **3** inches wide.

Thinking Kids' Math
Kindergarten
© Carson-Dellosa
CD-704461

149

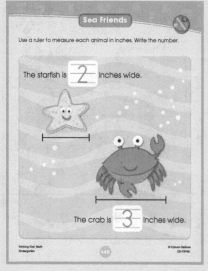

Sea Friends

Use a ruler to measure the animal in inches. Write the number.

The jellyfish is **5** inches long.

Thinking Kids' Math
Kindergarten
© Carson-Dellosa
CD-704461

150

Ready, Set, Go!

Use a ruler to measure each path around the track in inches. Write each number on the correct line.

6 in.

3 in.

7 in.

Thinking Kids' Math
Kindergarten
© Carson-Dellosa
CD-704461

151

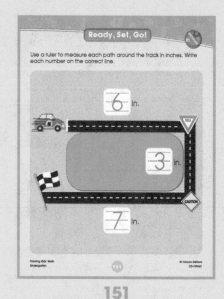

Doghouses

Measure each dog and doghouse in inches. Then, draw a line to connect each dog to the correct doghouse.

Thinking Kids' Math
Kindergarten
© Carson-Dellosa
CD-704461

152

Sorting Buttons

Put a button on each shirt that matches the color. Then, trace the color word.

yellow

red

Thinking Kids' Math
Kindergarten
© Carson-Dellosa
CD-704461

153

Sorting Buttons

Put a button on each shirt that matches the color. Then, trace the color word.

blue

green

Thinking Kids' Math
Kindergarten
© Carson-Dellosa
CD-704461

154

155

Sorting Buttons

Put a button on each shirt that matches the color. Then, trace the color word.

pink

orange

156

Roll or Stack?

Decide whether each figure will roll, stack, or do both. Circle each object that will roll. Draw an X on each object that will stack. Make a tally mark in the correct box or boxes.

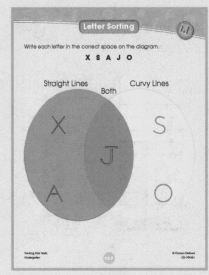

| Roll | |||| |
| Stack | ||||| |

157

Letter Sorting

Write each letter in the correct space on the diagram.

X S A J O

Straight Lines   Both   Curvy Lines

X
J
A
S
O

158

Letter Sorting

Write each letter in the correct space on the diagram.

U G K E M

Straight Lines   Both   Curvy Lines

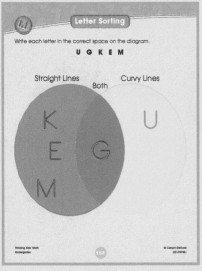

K
U
E G
M

159

Letter Sorting

Write each letter in the correct space on the diagram.

Q W C Z B

Straight Lines   Both   Curvy Lines

W
Q
C
Z
B

160

Butterfly Garden

Put matching colored buttons on each butterfly. Then, move the buttons onto the bar graph to graph the data.

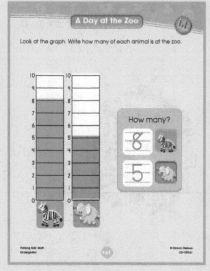

161

162

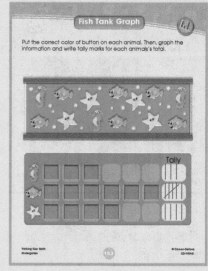

163

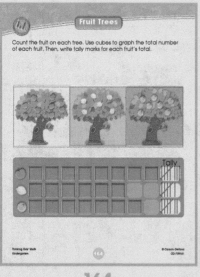

164

165